UNDERCURRENTS

LAST RIGHTS:
DEATH, DYING AND THE LAW IN IRELAND

UNDERCURRENTS

Other titles in the series

UNDERCURRENTS

Last Rights: Death, Dying and the Law in Ireland

PATRICK HANAFIN

CORK UNIVERSITY PRESS

First published in 1997 by
Cork University Press
University College
Cork
Ireland

British Library Cataloguing in Publication Data

A CIP catalogue record for this book is available from the British Library

ISBN 1 85918 156 2

Typeset by Seton Music Graphics, Bantry, Co. Cork
Printed by ColourBooks, Baldoyle, Co. Dublin

Contents

ACKNOWLEDGEMENTS

In the writing of this pamphlet I have received encouragement, support and criticism from many friends and colleagues. I would like to thank them all. My greatest intellectual debt is to Dr David Tomkin, whose commitment and wisdom guided me through the thesis from which the arguments in this pamphlet are drawn. Thanks also to Professor Vivien Hart and Professor Ian Ward for their support and encouragement.

1. Introduction

This pamphlet examines legal intervention in the area of death and dying. To what degree is it necessary or indeed acceptable to apply legal standards of fault and liability to the complex ethical problems which arise in the care of the terminally ill or incurable patient? What role should the law play in this field? Is there a consensus between the law's approach to this topic and that of the health-care provider?

A central theme is the idea of resolving the conflicting interests of the individual patient and the medical professional. In resolving any particular dilemma one must decide how much importance to give, on the one hand, to the autonomy of the individual patient and, on the other, to the freedom of the medical professional to intervene. Thus, the question can be framed in terms of the competing values of autonomy and the professionally perceived best interests of the individual.

It may seem particularly morbid to speak of attaining a state of not being, when the majority of human beings strive assiduously to avoid it. However, there are members of the human race for whom life is no longer an attractive alternative. The terminally ill person may consider death to be a release from a life consisting of pain and frustration. The individual who commits suicide has chosen death over a life which is filled with emotional or physical pain. Moreover, the person in a persistent vegetative state, though insentient and unable to choose, may, while conscious, have expressed a wish to die if she or he ever entered such a state.

In such instances, whether the person is competent or not, a decision must be made which will either lead to death or to continuing to live. This decision cannot be made in a vacuum. In arriving at the decision, one must take into account the legal and ethical consequences involved.

The pamphlet begins with an analysis of the way in which death is perceived in society, and how the institutions of medicine and the law have shaped our perception of death and how it should be confronted. The competing viewpoints on how far the law should impinge on individual autonomy are analysed in an attempt to discover the limits of legal intervention in this aspect of medical practice. From this general discussion, the work then moves on to the more specific application of law to the various aspects of death in the clinical context. Is it possible to discover particular ethical stances being reflected in legislation and judicial decisions in this area and, if so, to what extent does this affect the doctor–patient relationship?

The theoretical model on which this pamphlet is based is that of the ethical understanding of a right to life and in what circumstances, if ever, that right may be waived. When one speaks of the taking of life, one may initially think of equating it with such emotive synonyms as 'killing' and 'homicide'. Yet this is too simplistic a generalization of the issue. There may be particular extenuating circumstances, depending on the context in which the taking of life occurs. One cannot apply the same standards to the cold-blooded taking of life by, for example, a terrorist who places a bomb in a crowded shopping centre to the doctor who withdraws life-sustaining medical treatment from a patient in a persistent vegetative state based on the previously expressed wishes of the patient when in a sentient state.

However, there are those who will say that the taking of all human life, no matter at what stage of development, is murder. The pamphlet attempts to evaluate the competing arguments of those who are opposed to the taking of human life in all circumstances, and those who believe that there should be exceptions where the taking of life may be justified. The discussion then focuses on the question of legal responses to this issue, by looking at the differing legal reactions to active and passive euthanasia. How far does the autonomy of the individual extend? Can citizens be said to be truly autonomous if they are forbidden from exercising a right to die? Does such a right exist and, if so, in what circumstances may the individual exercise it? This issue allows one to examine the role of the health professional in contemporary society and the extent to which the Hippocratic tradition of life-preservation may be altered in the light of advances in medical technology.

In conclusion, the pamphlet suggests that a more patient-oriented approach should be taken by the law in the resolution of medical dilemmas. This would require a shift on the part of the law towards a model which views individual autonomy as being more important than the interests of the common good. An integral part of this development is the advancement of a more open and equal dialogue between all those concerned in this area of medical practice — health-care providers, patients and policy-makers.

2. THE MEDICO-LEGAL APPROPRIATION OF DEATH

Developments in medical technology have forced us, to a degree unimaginable even fifty years ago, to confront and question our ethical conceptions of the right to life and indeed of life itself. Technological changes have led to a gradual attitudinal shift in our ethical stance towards death and dying. In practical terms we can see a gradual appropriation of death by third parties, initially in the form of the medical profession, and more recently and as a corollary of the former, by the legal profession. The increasing technological complexity of medicine allows us to keep individuals alive artificially. This has led to a need to address in an ethical and legal sense the idea of life and when in fact it ends.

The genesis of scientific medicine in the nineteenth century prompted the transformation of the process of dying from an individual confrontation with mortality to an increasingly impersonal experience controlled by third parties in the form of health-care professionals. This monumental cultural shift from natural death to technological death has been described by Aries[1] as the move from the 'tame' death to the 'invisible' death. The 'tame' death is seen by Aries as part of a natural process. Death was accepted as part of the cycle of life. Once individuals know that their death is near, they do not rail against it but bow to the inevitable.

This death is marked by certain characteristics. Firstly, it announces its arrival in the form of a sign.[2] Once the individual has been made aware of his or her impending death a routine ritual took place. What Aries describes as the 'familiar simplicity' of this routine is the second characteristic of the 'tame' death. The individual, forewarned of his or her death, now goes about the uncomplicated process of dying. The third characteristic of the 'tame' death is the public character of such a way of dying. Death is viewed as a shared experience. The actor does not die alone in a hospital room. Rather, as Aries points out,

> Death was always public. Hence the profound signi-
> ficance of Pascal's remark that one dies alone, for at
> that time one was never physically alone at the moment
> of death. Today his statement has lost its impact, for
> one has a very good chance of literally dying alone, in
> a hospital room.[3]

Thus, death was ritualized, routinized and a collective experience.[4]

This model of death and dying was applicable in Ireland until relatively recent times.[5] However, today the tradition of 'waking' the dead has all but disappeared. This development has been ascribed variously to opposition from the Roman Catholic clergy[6] and the growth of the commercialization of death in the shape of the professional mortician.[7] Sheehy has outlined the advantages for the wider society in adhering to a model akin to the 'tame' death. The advantages accrue both to the bereaved and to the wider societal group:

> For the bereaved, traditional mourning rites and prac-
> tices of bereavement constitute a socially sanctioned
> and meaningful way of externalising the grief, frus-
> tration, anxiety and related responses experienced on
> the death of another. For the social group, it ensures
> that the psychologically disturbed state of the individual
> is rendered less harmful for the integrity of the on-
> going social order by permitting the bereaved person
> to indulge in what would otherwise be viewed as
> 'deviant' or unacceptable behaviour.[8]

Sheehy also notes that Irish culture has adopted a model of life as being endowed by a spiritual agent. There exists a natural cycle whereby life is regarded as coming from a sacred source, only to return to that source when life ends:

> Irish culture shares with many others a view that the
> life of an individual consists of a progression from a
> sacred, through a secular, to a sacred realm once more
> . . . Fundamental life crises have been ritualised in
> religion to a point where the primary ones are raised
> to the importance of highly significant social and
> spiritual events. Within Roman Catholic doctrine, for
> instance, five of the seven sacraments relate directly to
> times of transition in the life cycle . . .
>
> The ecclesiastic authority and symbolic role of
> the priest in the performance of these rituals is
> considerable. The part he plays and the symbols he
> manipulates are of the highest religious importance,

since he validates the 'passage rites' with the absolute power of divine presence. In this way, the divine elements validate significant transitions, including death, through the social order.[9]

The secularization of Irish society in recent times does not appear to have weakened the desire of individuals to engage in death ritual, albeit in a less intense manner than heretofore. Thus, as Sheehy concludes,

> The secularisation of Irish society and the commensurate weakening of institutionalised religion has changed the content and performance of death ritual but appears not to have diminished a commitment to it. The symbolic rites which integrate the culture of the living with the immutable ancestral culture of the dead . . . provide part of a social contract among the living in which death is given meaning through a reassurance of continued existence after dying, within the cultural and spiritual lineage of the dead and the vitality of the surviving order.[10]

The second model of death put forward by Aries is that of the 'invisible' death of contemporary society. This is the way we die today, intubated, unconscious in a hospital bed, divorced from our community. Death is viewed almost as a stigma, an evil to be avoided at all costs. This death has been facilitated by the advances in medical technology whereby the medical professional strives to overcome the reality of death by using a technological armoury. This is the death which has brought in its wake the increased interest of the legal profession, whether it be the courts in deciding whether a patient in a persistent vegetative state should be allowed to die or the legislature in introducing statutes to define death in a legal sense. Thus, as Aries sees it, the *locus* of death has been shifted from the home to the hospital, and with this geographical shift has come a shift in our conception of death:

> By a swift and imperceptible transition someone who was dying came to be treated like someone recovering from major surgery. This is why, especially in the cities, people stopped dying at home . . .
>
> The time of death can be lengthened to suit the doctor. The doctor cannot eliminate death, but he can control its duration, from the few hours it once was, to several days, weeks, months, or even years . . .
>
> Sometimes this prolonging of life becomes an end in itself, and hospital personnel refuse to discontinue the treatments that maintain an artificial life.[11]

The medicalization of death is the first step towards the need for legal intervention in this area. In the days of the 'tame' death it was quite straightforward. The individual died in the bosom of the community free from the interventions of third parties who used his or her body as a battleground in their war against mortality. Now, medicine has the ability to postpone the moment of death. This development has been accompanied by myriad legal complications which have brought the patient into another alien environment, that of the courtroom. Now that one can determine death by measuring brain waves, death has had to be redefined. Now that people live longer due to advances in disease-control, death does not come swiftly but is often slow and lingering. This leads to individuals asking to be relieved of this burden through active euthanasia or physician-assisted suicide. But is this not murder in the eyes of the law? Now that artificial respiration can keep accident victims alive indefinitely, the problem of when such intervention should cease arises. Is such cessation of treatment illegal? Death has been taken out of the hands of the dying. Instead, as Aries has put it,

> Death no longer belongs to the dying man, who is first irresponsible, later unconscious, nor to the family, who are convinced of their inadequacy. Death is regulated and organized by bureaucrats whose competence and humanity cannot prevent them from treating death as their 'thing', a thing that must bother them as little as possible in the general interest.[12]

With the medicalization of death came attendant legal problems. The focus of inquiry came to be placed on the surrounding circumstances of the individual's death rather than on the issue of death itself. It was no longer a simple question of knowing that you were about to die and accepting it calmly. Now that his or her destiny was in the hands of the medical profession it did not matter largely what the individual thought or knew, the medical professional always knew better. If an individual or a family tried to assert their independence in the matter by expressing a desire to be relieved of this prolonged life sentence, they were plunged into the even more clinical world of the legal professional. Despite the fact that the individual was employing the law as a means of obtaining what had previously been his or her death-right, the law further reified the individual. The *locus* was shifted to the even more alien and impersonal environment of the courtroom and the gap between individuals and their deaths was further widened by legal bureaucracy. Individuals' access to their own deaths had now to be secured through the instrumentality of legal professionals making death an even more impersonal and remote experience. Even though the law was establishing a right to die, two questions must be asked. Firstly, why did one, in the age of medicalized death, have to establish a right which had heretofore been well established in a cultural sense? Secondly, why was the legal process used to secure this right?

These questions may sound rather basic but they conceal far more than they reveal about the nature of individual autonomy in the context of medical death and the role of law in society. We can answer these questions superficially by saying that in such a case there is a conflict of values and opinions and that in such a conflictual situation the natural adjudicator is the judge. However, this does not answer the question of why, in a society which values individual autonomy, individuals have become so alienated from their bodies that they can no longer control their own deaths. Nor does it answer the question of the true role of law in society. Should law be concerned with intervening in a conflict so fundamental to individual autonomy as control over one's own life or death? In an ideal society the answer would be clear: the individual should be allowed to die naturally without the vain intervention of technology. However, we do not live in an ideal society and issues even as fundamental as this must be dealt with by surrogates, in this case the legal profession, rather than individuals themselves. In turn, the way in which the law and policy-makers deal with such issues is informed by various ethical views on life and death, thus further clouding the issue.

Daniel Callahan[13] has attempted to place this conundrum in a legal perspective. Callahan, while not altogether disagreeing with the way in which the law was used to (re-)establish a right to die, is not at the same time altogether happy with this approach. He believes that

> we have discovered in the language of choice and rights still another kind of evasion . . . . Faced with the possibility of going in different directions with death in the nineteen sixties and nineteen seventies, we collectively chose to add still another barrier between ourselves and a steady look at death; we chose 'choice' about death, rather than death itself, as the new, supposedly liberating focus. This was, at the time, a perfectly reasonable response. Many people were in

fact being denied a right to have treatment terminated, and a corrective was needed. It also served most effectively to stimulate public interest and discussion.

Death was, in a sense, taken out of the closet. But instead of being put forward for common thought and probing, it was put into the courtroom, turned into a matter of grand human rights.[14]

Callahan instead calls for a different response to the problem. Instead of placing the solution entirely in the hands of the law, cognizance must be taken of other aspects of society such as morality and cultural values. He thus points out that

there is an ever-present hazard in a culture that too easily mistakes the limited purpose of law for the broader and deeper demands of morality. It is that the aim of overcoming obstacles to choice to make way for meaning will be taken as the end of the matter, the latter task forgotten and slighted, culturally starved of the means of sustenance.[15]

Callahan proposes that the establishment of legal rights in the area of death is but a tiny contribution to the overall resolution of the problem. He is arguing for a context or a backdrop against which these rights can be exercised. He wants such rights to be 'undergirded by rich cultural and moral resources, and incentives to exercise that right wisely'.[16]

He is, in effect, arguing for the re-instatement of some form of moral code in society which gives, in his terms, another dimension to choices about death and dying. This dimension is the moral dimension. He notes that in abandoning the collective idea of a common destiny typical of the era of the 'tame' death, we have robbed death of its cultural significance and have been unable to find an enduring replacement. Thus, he claims

we do not have the shared sense of destiny that Phillipe
Aries identified as central to the possibility of a tame
death in an earlier time. We have tried, to be sure, to
find substitutes, but in each case they turn out to be
ways of better mastering and controlling death, not of
finding a common way to seek and share its meaning
and accept its inevitability.[17]

Callahan acknowledges that it may be rather difficult to return
to such a model but urges that we at least try. He sees a need to
re-evaluate the medical interpretation of death, to divest ourselves
of what he terms 'technological monism', by which he means 'the
tendency to erase the difference between human action as a cause
of what happens in the world, and independent, natural biological
processes, those old-fashioned causes of disease and death.'[18]

It is in this idea of 'technological monism' that we can begin to
see the reason why law has become increasingly involved in the
treatment of the dying. The move from seeing nature as the culpable party in the death of the individual to seeing the individual
medical professional as culpable has inevitably brought law, with
its ideas of fault and responsibility, into the scenario. As Callahan
puts it

Where once we human beings as moral agents stood
helpless in the face of nature, whose workings were
outside the range of our responsibility, now everything
is in some sense thought to be our responsibility.
Causality and culpability have been collapsed together.
The doctor who cannot save a patient faults her lack
of skill, or medicine's lack of a cure; it might have
been otherwise. The nurse who watches a feeding
tube removed from a hopelessly ill patient thinks the
patient is being killed by the removal, not by the
disease that made the tube necessary. The euthanasia

advocate holds that, by our adherence to a fictitious notion of 'allowing to die' from an underlying disease, we wilfully condemn a patient to needless suffering; direct killing would be more merciful, and the act of killing no different in any case from that of allowing to die. The euthanasia opponent, wary of badly motivated people using nature and its ways as an excuse, comes to see culpability in the movement to make allowing to die easier.[19]

On this analysis it can be seen that the move from the 'tame' death to the invisible or medicalized death has brought with it the need for greater legal involvement in the dying process.

The involvement of the law is twofold. Firstly, there is the intervention of constitutional law with its notions of individual rights. This is used to establish within the new model of death a right to die, employing terms such as a right to privacy or autonomy or choice. Secondly, there is the intervention of the criminal law, with its notions of fault and responsibility. This is used to regulate the behaviour of the individual medical professional, based on the premise that it is the actions of the medical professional, and not the disease, as was previously the case, which cause the death of the individual patient.

This pamphlet examines the way in which law intervenes in the medical treatment of death and dying in order to establish whether, and to what extent, such intervention is either necessary or effective. Should we merely view death as a question of rights or is there some other way in which the conflict between a 'tame' death and medical intervention can be resolved? Moreover, is the intervention of the criminal law in this area based on a mistaken premise? Is there any need for such intervention in the area of medical treatment? If not, what alternative models should be applied? In addition it will be necessary to analyse the various practical ramifications of the theoretical models which have informed the legal debate on the taking of life to date, with a view to testing their validity and the contribution, if any, which they can make to the resolution of the problem.

3. COMPETING MORAL AND CULTURAL PERSPECTIVES

On the theoretical plane there are diverse conceptions of the right to life, ranging from the view that all life is sacred and should not be taken in any circumstances, to those who believe that there are circumstances in which the right to life may be waived. The following section attempts to evaluate the competing arguments of those who are opposed to the taking of human life in all circumstances, and those who believe that there should be exceptions where the taking of life may be justified.

The purpose of this exercise is to link the diverse policy stances and attitudes which shall be encountered in subsequent chapters to particular philosophical traditions. To fully understand why there is such a deep division in society over the questions of life, death and dying, one must be acquainted with the ethical models which influence these diverse viewpoints.

The sanctity of life model holds that all instances of deliberate killing of an innocent human being are morally wrong. This conception of killing falls into what Ronald Dworkin has referred to as a 'duty-based' moral view.[20] This model, however, allows for certain exceptions where the taking of life may be deemed to be justified. Thus, acts which do not have as their primary motivation the killing of another, but nonetheless lead to his or her death, may be justified. This category of exceptions includes such acts as killing in self-defence[21] and pregnancy termination which results indirectly from attempts to save the life of the mother who is suffering from uterine cancer. This argument was later to be adapted by Roman Catholic theologians to form the basis of the doctrine of double effect.[22] The doctrine of double effect would allow for an exception to the sanctity of life model of the right to life when it can be determined that the intention of the individual was not to kill but to bring about some other result such as the curing of pain. Thus, for example, Roman Catholic moral teaching would allow for an exception to the moral prohibition on killing in a case where a doctor intended to alleviate a patient's pain by administering a pain-killing drug, but this intentional act had the unintended side effect or double effect of killing the patient.[23] A second category of exceptions is based on the idea that the intentional taking of life in certain circumstances may be justified. Thus, in the case of capital punishment, the execution of a murderer is seen as justified on the grounds that he or she has transgressed a basic moral principle and has therefore forfeited the right to life.[24] Moreover, in the case of killing in war, the defence of one's country or some justifiable cause is seen as sufficient justification for the intentional killing of others.[25]

Thus, on the whole, this approach to the question of taking life tends to an absolutist view, leaving aside the exceptions which are included in the model. The element of individual choice or autonomy has no place in this moral view. As Dworkin has written, in adverting to the general category of duty-based moral theories, such a model is concerned with the moral quality of an individual's acts and supposes 'that it is wrong, without more, for an individual to fail to meet certain standards of behaviour'.[26]

The primary source of Irish law, *Bunreacht na hÉireann* 1937, owes a large debt to this view of morality, for it is from such a duty-based moral view that the Constitution derives its theoretical underpinning.[27] One need look no further than the Preamble to the Constitution to discover its Thomist nature. Thus, the Constitution is enacted in the name of 'the Most Holy Trinity, from Whom is all authority and to Whom, as our final end, all actions both of men and states may be referred'. As one commentator has noted, the Preamble makes clear

> that the Constitution and the laws which owe their force to the Constitution derive, under God, from the people and are directed to the promotion of the common good. If a judicial decision rejects the divine law or has not as its object the common good, it has not the character of law. This idea is no strange addition to the common law; it is as old as Coke.[28]

The implications of such a philosophical model for the way in which the law views the taking of life are of fundamental importance here. In subsequent chapters the practical legal ramifications of this philosophical stance for issues such as treatment withdrawal, active euthanasia and physician-assisted suicide are examined in order to discover if the presence in the Constitution of such a philosophical model has had a bearing on the way in which these issues are dealt with in practice.

It is submitted that the argument against taking the life of the unborn may be applied *mutatis mutandis* to the question of the taking of life in the case of the terminally ill or incurable patient. As with abortion, the sanctity of life model admits of exceptions to this general prohibition, again based on a variant of the doctrine of double effect, where, for example, the doctor intended a 'good' end, the easing of pain, but in the process 'indirectly' caused the death of the patient.

The attitude which one adopts to the place of the natural law in Irish jurisprudence will have implications for individual autonomy in areas which fall within the category of the taking of life. Due to the special significance afforded to the right to life in duty-based moral views, the scope for individual autonomy in relation to the taking of life in the medical context will be severely curtailed.

Thus, if as certain commentators claim,[29] all positive laws must ultimately defer to the supremacy of the natural or divine law, then the outcome in practical legal terms will be a severe curtailment of the right to die.[30] As one of those commentators, Justice Declan Costello, pointed out, while writing extrajudicially, if it is necessary for the court to determine the nature of the individual who is the subject of certain constitutional rights, then

> the courts can properly ascertain that nature in the light of the Christian revelation which the Constitution proclaims the people to have accepted . . . it can clearly be inferred that the Constitution rejects legal positivism as a basis for the protection of fundamental rights, and suggests instead a theory of natural law from which these rights can be derived.[31]

Such an argument assumes that the Constitution as enacted in 1937 recognizes the superiority of the divine or natural law and as such any legal provisions, or for that matter constitutional amendments which conflict with the ideals of natural law, are invalid even if they are technically in agreement with the provisions of the Constitution.

This is the argument put forward by Roderick O'Hanlon, when he claims that the constitutional mechanism of consulting the people on issues of constitutional importance may not be entirely appropriate in all circumstances.[32] He was advancing this argument against the backdrop of the decision of the Supreme Court in the case of *Attorney General v X and Others*[33] and the subsequent referendums on the issues of pregnancy termination, the right to travel and the right to information. Roderick O'Hanlon framed the question in the following terms:

> Is there any limitation on the power in Article 46.1 of the Constitution by which '[a]ny provision of this Constitution may be amended'?
> This question goes to the root of the nature of law. It obliges us to consider the relationship between basic human rights and the process of political resolution of issues of public controversy.[34]

The manner in which O'Hanlon answers this question is influenced by his conception of law, a conception which fits quite comfortably into the natural law model. He is thus able to claim that the Constitution is based on precepts of natural law and, as such, these precepts should be adhered to 'so long as they remain part of the Constitution'.[35]

O'Hanlon's conclusions are of relevance to the subject matter of this pamphlet in that they constitute a major argument against the liberalization of laws in relation to the treatment of the terminally ill or incurable patient. His conception of rights tends to view the right to life as absolute, except in a number of exceptional circumstances which accord with Roman Catholic teaching. If one were to accept his argument that the Constitution may only be interpreted in the light of natural law doctrine, and in particular, the classical model of this doctrine as espoused by Thomas Aquinas and adopted by the Roman Catholic Church, then one limits the autonomy of individuals to choose to act in accordance with their own wishes rather than in accordance with a moral code. Thus, O'Hanlon is able to arrive at the following conclusions as to which rights are to be valued in society:

> It is universally accepted that the most fundamental of all human rights is the right to life. The most elementary

> and universal aspect of this right is the right not to be
> killed for the sake of another or for some further end.
> This right is enjoyed equally by all human beings at all
> times. It is attacked whenever abortion, murder or
> euthanasia are practised.[36]

The argument that any piece of legislation, constitutional amendment or judicial decision which was in conflict with the natural or divine law would be invalid seems to depart entirely both from legal reality and logic. Thus, a statute such as the Criminal Justice (Sexual Offences) Act 1993 which decriminalized homosexual acts between consenting males over the age of seventeen, the decision of the Supreme Court in the case of *Attorney General v X and Others*[37] where it was held that pregnancy termination was lawful to save the life as opposed to the health of the mother in a case involving a fourteen-year-old rape victim who was pregnant as a result, and the subsequent amendments to the Constitution on the rights to travel and information are all invalid according to O'Hanlon's vision of the protection of human rights and of law in general. According to O'Hanlon's conception of individual rights it is quite acceptable to treat individuals differently in the eyes of the law because of their sexual orientation, to brand them as criminals because of what they are and tacitly endorse discrimination against such individuals, to prevent individuals from moving freely outside of the jurisdiction, and to prevent individuals from obtaining access to information which is freely accessible in other states and which may affect other rights such as their right to privacy and their right to medical treatment.

One could extend this view further to other aspects of personal autonomy which come into conflict with the right to life as understood by the natural law model. Thus, under O'Hanlon's view of human rights, an incurably ill patient could be prevented from being assisted to die by his or her medical practitioner, from requesting that his or her life be terminated by lethal injection to cut short the indignity of lying in his or her own excrement and being fed through a drip. Moreover, an incurably ill patient could be prevented from exercising the right to travel out of this jurisdiction to a country where the practice of physician-assisted suicide or active voluntary euthanasia is not outlawed.

In practice we have seen that the Supreme Court has not been so absolutist in its interpretation of the Constitution. This seems to lead one to the tentative conclusion that the interpretation of a constitution is not as clear-cut as O'Hanlon would argue and that in accepting the philosophical bases of the Constitution one does not have to accept blindly a set of moral dogma into the bargain. This is to be plainly construed from the interpretation of the American Constitution which was also inspired by the ideals of natural rights.[38] However, this fact did not constrict the Supreme Court in the United States from adopting a model of constitutional interpretation which was far from absolutist.[39]

One must remember that at the time of the introduction of the American Constitution the franchise did not extend beyond property-owning males and that slave-ownership was condoned. Are we to remain constricted in our efforts to improve the lot of humanity by adhering to a petrified constitutional document? Or are we to allow such a document to be expressive of the rights and interests of all citizens equally?

One could conclude that the meaning of a constitution is dependent on the theoretical model which is applied to it by the reigning polity (including the judiciary). Under the model proposed by O'Hanlon, one can see what Feldman has referred to as an 'uncritical commitment to a sacred text',[40] and what Ronald Dworkin has referred to as a 'constitution of detail'.[41] Thus, the right to life is seen as more fundamental than other equally valid rights and is adhered to even when it would interfere greatly with the autonomy of the individual. This is the traditional Irish model.

This is also the view adopted by religious and conservative thinkers who claim that there exists a certain natural order of things which must be adhered to. Any form of behaviour which does not conform to this ideal is immediately viewed as suspect.

This, however, is not the only model of the Constitution. As Dworkin's critique implies, there are equally valid theoretical models which may be used as the basis for our conceptualization of the role of law in society. The rights-based moral view differs from deontological models in that the focus is on individual rights rather than duties.[42] According to Dworkin, rights-based models are concerned with 'the independence rather than the conformity of individual action. They presuppose and protect the value of individual thought and choice.'[43] As Brock has noted,

> Rights function differently than duties in that they delineate areas in which the person possessing the right is at liberty to act as he sees fit and to act in his own interest as he understands it, as opposed to delineating specific constraints to which he must conform.[44]

Moreover, within the rights model the individual is deemed to be free from interference in the exercise of his right. It could therefore be looked upon as a model which respects above all else the principle of individual autonomy. Thus, as Brock observes,

> Rights-based views emphasize a view of persons as capable of forming purposes, of making plans, of weighing alternatives according to how well they fulfil those plans and purposes, and of acting on the basis of this deliberation. Rights protect our exercise of these capacities whose exercise is often associated with the notion of autonomy, independent of how doing so promotes goals specified as valuable.[45]

Applying this model to the question of the taking of life, one can state that an individual has a right to life unless and until he/she waives that right. However, in waiving that right the individual must act voluntarily and be capable of waiving that right. Thus, on a rights analysis the taking of life is morally wrong when that life is taken without the right-holder having waived that right.

However, if the right-holder has validly waived his or her right not to be killed then the rights view will not hold the taking of life in such circumstances to be morally wrong. Brock[46] outlines the possible consequences of applying the rights model by detailing two different scenarios in the medical context. In the first scenario, a patient is suffering from a terminal and incurable disease, as a result of which she is unable to lead a normal life. The patient is expected to die from this disease within a year. In addition, she has no friends or relatives who care about her. She makes it known that everything be done to keep her alive for as long as possible, despite the expense of this treatment. Due to certain unique features of her condition, if she is killed now it is likely that new medical knowledge will be obtained that will enable the suffering of similar patients to be alleviated.[47] In applying the rights-based model to this scenario, Brock concludes that the taking of the life of this patient would be morally wrong as she has neither waived, forfeited or failed to exercise her right not to be killed.[48]

In the second scenario Brock cites the following example:

> Smith has terminal, incurable cancer. It completely prevents him from leading a normal life, causes him considerable though not unbearable pain and suffering, and he is expected to die from it in roughly a year. His treatment is expensive, but such that his family can afford it without undue stress. Smith is fully in control of his rational faculties, has given long and serious thought to his situation, and has decided

he wants to die because life in his present condition is
not worth living. He is unable, in his present situation,
to bring about his own death, and requests another
. . . to do so. He will only die if steps directly
intended to kill him are taken.[49]

If one were to apply the rights-based model to this case then
it would be morally permissible to take Smith's life. This is so
because Smith has waived his right not to be killed by asking for
his life to be terminated, and is competent to do so.

Therefore, it can be seen that the particular model which one
adopts in approaching the topic of the taking of life in the medical
context will have a practical bearing on the decision arrived at in
each particular case. The implications of each of these models for
patient autonomy are examined in the chapters which follow.

4. ENDLESS LIFE: TREATMENT

WITHDRAWAL

Passive euthanasia consists of refraining from taking all steps necessary to keep a terminally ill patient or a patient in a persistent
vegetative state alive. A more formal and comprehensive definition
would be that provided by Pieter Admiraal who defines it as 'the
conscious decision by a doctor either to discontinue an existing
treatment or not to initiate treatment, as a result of which the
patient dies after a shorter or longer period.'[50] However, while on
the surface the definition of passive euthanasia may appear unprob-
lematic, in practice this is far from the case. Thus, in the case of a
patient whose life is being sustained by means of a respirator, does
turning off the respirator constitute a positive act or an omission?

Many would argue that the withdrawal of the respirator is a positive act and therefore is tantamount to killing the patient. Indeed, as will be argued later in this chapter, the tenuous distinction between active and passive euthanasia complicates rather than clarifies the euthanasia debate. As Mason has noted, the term passive euthanasia

> is falling into disuse and is excluded from the Dutch definition of euthanasia. Arguably a preferable terminology is selective non-treatment . . . It almost goes without saying that, if the object of one's action or inaction is the death of one's patient, it is irrelevant as to intention whether one adopts passive or active means to that end.[51]

Despite the chimeric nature of the distinction between active and passive means of euthanasia, the law continues to adhere to this rather unhelpful formulation. As Lord Browne-Wilkinson observed in his judgment in the House of Lords decision in *Airedale N.H.S. Trust v Bland*,[52]

> the conclusion I have reached will appear to some to be almost irrational. How can it be lawful to allow a patient to die slowly, though painlessly, over a period of weeks from lack of food but unlawful to produce his immediate death by a lethal injection, thereby saving his family from yet another ordeal to add to the tragedy that has already struck them? I find it difficult to find a moral answer to that question. But it is undoubtedly the law and nothing I have said casts doubt on the proposition that the doing of a positive act with the intention of ending life is and remains murder.[53]

This topic has become the subject of widespread debate in recent years. In the United States, Canada, the United Kingdom,

New Zealand and latterly in Ireland the courts have been forced to make pronouncements on the issue. What can be seen from the various judicial and legislative developments in the last twenty years is a general acceptance of a right not to have one's life maintained artificially. This chapter attempts to delineate the boundaries of any future legislative intervention on this issue and to outline the options available to the judiciary in coming to a decision in this area.

Arguably, the act–omission distinction appears to be more of a hindrance than an aid to resolving the legal problems in this area. It is more in the way of a legal fiction designed to elude a definitive resolution of the issue than a positive contribution towards the resolution of the problem.

This view was well put in an anonymous note in the *Harvard Law Review*.[54] The author, in arguing against distinctions between acts and omissions in the case of physician-assisted suicide and treatment refusal, states

> Because there are no inherent distinctions between letting a patient die and assisting a patient's suicide, the patient's interest in dying cannot, without implicating policy arguments, be divided into an interest in 'refusing' and an interest in 'receiving' treatment. The patient has a single, undivided interest in controlling what happens to her body. The right of self-determination, although subject to some overriding state interests, does not cease to exist at some indeterminate, imaginary line between having life-saving treatment withdrawn and receiving suicide assistance . . .
>
> Legal causation is a question of policy, not mechanical connection. Consider a case in which a physician disconnects a respirator that is keeping a patient alive. If the patient had expressly requested continued treatment, surely a court would find that the physician's act

caused the patient's death. However, the same act would be legal if the patient had demanded cessation of treatment. In either case, the physician's act – turning off the respirator – is a cause-in-fact of the death: but for turning off the machine, the patient would be alive today. To say that the physician did not cause the death of the patient who demanded withdrawal of treatment, then, means that this act was not the legal, or 'proximate' cause of the death. Whether the physician's act is a proximate cause 'depend[s] essentially on whether the policy of the law will extend the responsibility for the conduct to the consequences which have in fact occurred' . . . Thus, the seemingly objective statement that would be made in the second instance, that the patient's illness, not the patient or the physician, caused the death, is no more than a policy-based conclusion that the patient's and physician's actions are not prohibited.[55]

Thus, the act–omission distinction is a shaky foundation on which to build a right-to-die jurisprudence. It could be argued that it is an outmoded legal tool unsuited to the exigencies of high-technology medicine.[56] As a result, it is submitted that other models be looked to in attempting to seek a resolution to this dilemma.

One commentator who has elaborated on the act–omission argument in the context of Irish law is Justice Declan Costello. In an article on the issue of refusal of medical treatment,[57] Justice Costello argued that

the dignity and autonomy of the human person (as constitutionally predicated) require the [s]tate to recognise that decisions relating to life and death are, generally speaking, ones which a competent adult should be free to make without outside restraint and that this freedom should be regarded as an aspect of the right to privacy which should be protected as a 'personal' right by Article 40.3.1.[58]

However, he goes on to state that such a right is not absolute. Thus, he states that if one is to define a right to die as a

> 'right' to procure death by his or her [the patient's] hand or by means of someone else, then it cannot be said that there is a constitutionally protected 'right to die', for it is a reasonable conclusion from the nature of man as envisaged in the Constitution that he may not kill himself or ask others to assist him to do so.[59]

Nonetheless, he states that one can make a distinction between the above conception of the right to die and the concept of allowing the patient to die by discontinuing life-sustaining treatment. Justice Costello provides the following rationale for this position:

> In the case of the competent patient discontinuance would be in response to a request which the patient was constitutionally entitled to make, and no 'unlawful' act would occur. In the case of the incompetent patient discontinuance in the proper discharge of a duty of care would likewise involve no legal fault and the patient's death could not be an 'unlawful' homicide.[60]

This argument is yet another example of that nebulous act–omission distinction which has less to do with an adherence to logic than with a casuistical argument based on a particular philosophical perspective.

There are those who contend that such a distinction is chimeric and that there is indeed no moral distinction between killing and letting die. James Rachels[61] argues against this distinction. He claims that

> The bare difference between killing and letting die does not, in itself, make a moral difference. If a doctor lets a patient die for humane reasons, he is in the same moral position as if he had given the patient a lethal injection for humane reasons. If his decision was wrong – if, for example, the patient's illness was in fact curable – the decision would be equally regrettable no matter which method was used to carry it out. And if the doctor's decision was the right one, the method used was not in itself important.[62]

In arguing in this fashion Rachels attempts to arrive at the conclusion that if one is to justify killing in one instance, such as in the case of treatment withdrawal, then one should logically justify killing in the case of active euthanasia. He goes on to cite the typical argument against such a stance, an argument substantially similar to that of Justice Costello:

> The important difference between active and passive euthanasia is that, in passive euthanasia, the doctor does not do anything to bring about the patient's death. The doctor does nothing, and the patient dies of whatever ills already afflict him. In active euthanasia, however, the doctor does something to bring about the patient's death: he kills him. The doctor who gives the patient with cancer a lethal injection has himself caused his patient's death; whereas if he merely ceases treatment, the cancer is the cause of death.[63]

Rachels argues that such a distinction carries no moral weight. He argues that a decision to withdraw treatment is subject to moral appraisal in the same way that a decision to kill . . . would be subject to moral appraisal: it may be assessed as wise or unwise, compassionate or sadistic, right or wrong. If a doctor deliberately lets a patient die who was suffering from a routinely curable illness, the doctor would certainly be to blame for what he had done, just as he would be to blame if he had needlessly killed the patient.[64]

Thus, if it is possible to state that there is no difference between killing and letting die and that in effect what one is doing in both cases is 'killing', why do commentators such as Costello argue so vehemently in favour of treatment withdrawal and so vehemently against active euthanasia? Is there a basis other than logic upon which they base their arguments? To discover the motivation of such arguments one must examine the foundations of the act–omission distinction.

Feinberg has placed such arguments into the category of the 'moral significance claim'.[65] Simply put, the moral significance claim attempts to demonstrate that there is a difference between causing something to happen and merely allowing that thing to happen and that this difference is morally significant. It is significant enough, Feinberg adds, 'to warrant imposing criminal liability for those who intentionally cause certain harms while withholding criminal liability from those who merely fail to prevent those harms when they can.'[66] This in effect is what Justice Costello is claiming.

Can such a claim be justified? Rachels, in his argument, would answer in the negative. There is no significant moral difference between killing and letting die.

In the Irish context, the act–omission distinction in itself may not be morally significant. Rather, what is of significance for those like Justice Costello who put forward such an argument are other factors. Thus, for example, given the specific symbolic, cultural and legal significance given to the right to life in Ireland, it would not be fallacious to infer that in the context of treatment withdrawal the distinction is being used as a casuistical tool to prevent one from conflicting with the ideal of the sanctity of life. By stating that the withdrawal of treatment is less morally reprehensible than killing, Justice Costello stays within the boundaries of the sanctity of life argument. If he were to do otherwise he would leave the door wide open for the justification of active euthanasia, a far greater evil than mere treatment withdrawal under his model. Rather, this concession to patient autonomy could be regarded as a strategic ploy, a battle lost in order to win the war for the sanctity of life.

If one accepts the view that there is no morally significant difference between killing and letting die, that they are, in fact, both species of killing, then one has to ask the entirely separate question, in what circumstances is killing justifiable? This allows one to look at the individual cases free of the haze of moral certitude. It also entails altering radically perceived societal beliefs in relation to the concept of killing. This requires an adjustment to the traditional sanctity of life model, by moving to a less absolutist position on the right to life.

By adopting the formulation advanced by commentators such as Rachels, we are confronting the problem rather than sliding across it on a thin layer of casuistry. One can then accept that both treatment withdrawal and more active means of hastening death are not morally separable, that they are both acts of killing. However, we can then progress to the next plane of argument and state that even though these acts may be classified as killing they are not necessarily without justification. We do not have to place a moral overlay on such acts and condemn them as absolutely evil and beyond the pale of human behaviour.

Thus, Justice Costello's argument is not as clear-cut as it might appear at first glance. His analysis of the right to die – even though it in some way recognizes the patient as an autonomous agent – is not, however, an ideal solution. Individual patients may only exercise their right to die in limited circumstances, that is, only when no active measures are used to hasten a patient's death. This is not a right to die in the true sense of the word but a *conditional* right to die. One cannot choose the manner of one's death without restriction. This type of argument is loaded with contradiction. One has a right to die but only if there is no 'active' intervention by a third party or assistance from a third party which could constitute aiding, abetting, counselling or procuring a suicide. If one is suffering from terminal cancer or AIDS, is conscious of one's pain and suffering, and has the lack of good fortune not to be an unconscious coma victim requiring artificial feeding and hydration, then one cannot choose to hasten one's end. Thus, self-determination in this instance is only afforded to those who cannot exercise it, whereas those who can may not, due to their wishes interfering with the 'natural order' of things.

In Ireland, the issue of treatment withdrawal finally came before the courts for adjudication in 1995 in the case of *Re a Ward of Court*.[67] In this case the ward was a forty-five-year-old woman who at the age of twenty-two had suffered irreversible brain damage during a minor surgical procedure under general anaesthetic. This left her in a near persistent vegetative state and she had been kept alive since the mishap by means of artificial hydration and nutrition. At first this was delivered by means of a naso-gastric tube but for the last three years food and water had been delivered by means of a gastronomy tube going directly through her abdomen wall into her stomach.

The ward was unable to communicate. She had minimal capacity to recognize nursing staff and to react to strangers by showing signs of distress. She was able to follow people with her eyes in a reflex manner. Her family was of the opinion that it was in her 'best interests' that she be allowed to die naturally.

Accordingly, the family applied to the High Court for an order directing artificial nutrition and hydration to cease, where the application was heard by Justice Lynch. The institution in which the ward resided objected to such an order, claiming that it was contrary to its ethical code.

Justice Lynch was of the opinion that in the case of an incompetent, incurably ill patient, the health-care provider in question, may, subject to the acquiesence of the next-of-kin, lawfully withdraw life-sustaining medical treatment or refrain from providing such treatment. In this case the health-care providers objected to this withdrawal of treatment. Justice Lynch held that in such a case the test to be applied is whether it is in the 'best interests' of the patient that her life should be prolonged by artificial means. Justice Lynch also took into account what would be the patient's own wishes if she could be granted a momentary lucid period. The judge concluded that the courts in such cases should 'approach the matter from the standpoint of a prudent, good and loving parent in deciding what course should be adopted'.[68] In this regard the test which Justice Lynch applied was a hybrid one. He set out the test in the following terms: 'Whilst the best interests of the Ward is the acid test, I think that I can take into account what would be her own wishes if she could be granted a momentary lucid and articulate period in which to express them . . .'[69]

The matter was appealed to the Supreme Court by the Attorney General, the institution, and the guardian *ad litem* on behalf of the ward. In the Supreme Court the order of Justice Lynch in the High Court was upheld. While favouring the order, the Supreme Court tended more to applying a discrete 'best interests' test rather than the hybrid model favoured by Justice Lynch. This does not necessarily rule out the application of the substituted judgement test in later cases where it may be deemed appropriate to do so.

It could be suggested that at first sight the 'best interests' standard may be rather objective in nature, in that it does not focus on how the patient would have chosen, if capable of so doing, but rather on the decision which is most in keeping with the welfare of the patient. The 'best interests' test as applied to treatment withdrawal has been defined as follows:

> In assessing whether a procedure or course of treatment would be in a patient's 'best interests', the surrogate must take into account such factors as the relief of suffering, the preservation or restoration of functioning, and the quality as well as the extent of life sustained.[70]   .

The 'best interests' standard has its origins in the equitable jurisdiction to oversee the estates of incompetents.[71] The application of this standard to the field of medical decision-making is well established. Thus, it is used to justify decisions to treat individuals who may not be capable to consent to such treatment, such as children[72] and people with a mental handicap.[73] However, in the United States the 'best interests' standard has not been applied very frequently in the area of treatment withdrawal. As one commentator has noted,

> In right to die cases, however, the courts have generally concluded that medical treatment does not always advance a person's interests. This is evidenced by the fact that competent patients sometimes refuse treatment, even life-sustaining treatment and, when there are no countervailing state interests of a compelling nature, that refusal is to be accorded the same respect that a patient's consent to treatment is accorded.[74]

Certain courts have, however, applied the 'best interests' test in such cases. Thus, in the California Court of Appeal decision in In Re Conservatorship of Drabnick,[75] it was held that a statutorily appointed conservator should decide the issue of treatment withdrawal in the case of an incompetent patient, who had not made a formal advance directive, on the basis of the 'best interests' standard. In the Minnesota case of *In Re Torres*[76] the 'best interests' test was also applied. It was noted in that case that one factor that should be taken into account was the welfare of the surviving family. However, it has been argued that this standard strays too far away from the ideal of patient autonomy and that indeed one may be confusing other interests with the 'best interests' of the patient:

> To the extent that most patients have an interest in the well-being of their family, advancing the interests of their family benefits them as well. Importing such considerations into the 'best interests' analysis, however, invites the conflicts of interest that plague the 'substituted judgement' standard and risks shifting the focus of inquiry to the 'best interests' of the family.[77]

The 'best interests' test has fared rather more successfully in other jurisdictions in relation to treatment withdrawal. In the United Kingdom the judiciary was faced with the problem of how to decide for the incompetent patient in the case of *Airedale N.H.S. Trust v Bland*.[78] The case concerned Tony Bland who, at the age of seventeen, was seriously injured in the Hillsborough football disaster in 1989. He suffered brain damage which left him in a persistent vegetative state. The condition was described thus by the Master of the Rolls, Sir Thomas Bingham in his judgment in the Court of Appeal decision on the case:

> the brain-stem remains alive and functioning while the cortex of the brain loses its function and activity. Thus the P.V.S. patient continues to breathe unaided and his

digestion continues to function. But although his eyes are open, he cannot see. He cannot hear. Although capable of reflex movement, particularly in response to painful stimuli, the patient is incapable of voluntary movement and can feel no pain. He cannot taste or smell. He cannot speak or communicate in any way. He has no cognitive function and can thus feel no emotion, whether pleasure or distress. The absence of cerebral function is not a matter of surmise; it can be scientifically demonstrated. The space which the brain should occupy is full of watery fluid.[79]

The manner in which the House of Lords addressed the problem at issue is reflective of the 'best interests' approach. Indeed, the 'substituted judgement' approach as developed by United States courts in the case of the incompetent and non-sentient patient was explicitly rejected by Lord Mustill in his judgment in *Airedale N.H.S. Trust v Bland*.[80]

In referring to the 'best interests' test as previously used in a rather controversial manner by the House of Lords in the case of *Re F (Mental Patient: Sterilisation)*,[81] a case involving an application for the non-voluntary sterilization of a mentally handicapped woman, and applying it to the facts in the *Bland* case, Their Lordships came to the conclusion that the 'best interests' of the patient dictated termination of life-sustaining medical treatment.[82] In the words of Lord Browne-Wilkinson, the correct manner in which the dilemma in such cases should be posed is as follows:

> The critical decision to be made is whether it is in the 'best interests' of Anthony Bland to continue the invasive medical care involved in artificial feeding. That question is not the same as, 'Is it in Anthony Bland's "best interests" that he should die?' The latter question assumes that it is lawful to perpetuate the

patient's life: but such perpetuation of life can only be achieved if it is lawful to continue to invade the bodily integrity of the patient by invasive medical care. Unless the doctor has reached the affirmative conclusion that it is in the patient's best interest to continue the invasive care, such care must cease.[83]

Lord Mustill also framed the question in such terms when he stated that the focus of inquiry should be placed on the 'interests of the patient, not in the termination of life but in the continuation of his treatment'.[84] Lord Mustill went on to delineate the boundaries of the 'best interests' test in such a case as follows:

> (i) The cessation of nourishment and hydration is an omission not an act. (ii) Accordingly, the cessation will not be a criminal act unless the doctors are under a present duty to continue the regime. (iii) At the time when Anthony Bland came into the care of the doctors decisions had to be made about his care which he was unable to make for himself. In accordance with *Re F (Mental Patient: Sterilisation)* [1989] 2 All E.R. 545 these decisions were to be made in his 'best interests'. Since the possibility that he might recover still existed his 'best interests' required that he should be supported in the hope that this would happen. These 'best interests' justified the application of the necessary regime without his consent. (iv) All hope of recovery has now been abandoned. Thus, although the termination of his life is not in the 'best interests' of Anthony Bland, his 'best interests' in being kept alive have also disappeared, taking with them the justification for the non-consensual regime and the co-relative duty to be kept in being. (v) Since there is no longer a duty to provide nourishment and hydration a failure to do so cannot be a criminal offence.[85]

The 'best interests' test, conversely to the United States, is thus the favoured test in Irish and English treatment-withdrawal cases. However, Ian Kennedy and Andrew Grubb[86] do not share the opinion that the 'substituted judgement' test is not applicable in such cases. They claim that the 'substituted judgement' test is a better protector of individual self-determination, whereas the 'best interests' test does not place as high a value on the concept of self-determination. In their opinion:

> It is not clear whether Lord Mustill intended to banish the 'substituted judgement' test from English law completely. He suggested that it could be applied where the patient is sentient but unable to communicate and hence is incompetent to make a decision. If this is correct, he contradicts himself. For, if the test is applicable to that case, it is applicable even though it is a 'fiction'. In principle, the decision-maker cannot know any more than in a case where the patient is unconscious. In both cases the decision-maker is required to ask himself 'what would the patient want?'. The patient cannot help him any more than if he were unconscious. Thus, in both cases all will turn on the extent to which the patient has made his wishes known.
>
> In our view, it is still open for English law to adopt this more sophisticated approach of seeking to apply 'substituted judgement' before having recourse to 'best interests' where it is appropriate. The form the law would take would be that the doctor's duty is first to consider what he believes would be the patient's decision and only secondly, in default of that, to fall back on the 'best interests' test.[87]

The 'substituted judgement' test allows the surrogate to choose the course which most closely approximates to the patient's own wishes based on such factors as the probable effects of continued treatment, the likelihood of a cure, and the patient's views, if any, on life-sustaining treatment expressed while competent.[88] This test has been defined in the following terms:

> The doctrine of 'substituted judgement' . . . was utilized to authorize a gift from the estate of an incompetent person to an individual when the incompetent owed no duty of support. The English court accomplished this purpose by substituting itself as nearly as possible for the incompetent, and acting on the same motives and considerations as would have moved him . . . In essence, the doctrine in its original inception called on the court to 'don the mantle of the incompetent'.[89]

The test as originally articulated was applicable only to the distribution of funds from the estates of the mentally incompetent by the court of chancery exercising its *parens patriae* jurisdiction. However, it was adapted for use in a most inappropriate manner by the New Jersey Supreme Court in the case of *In Re Quinlan*.[90] In this case, the patient Karen Quinlan was seventeen years old and was in a permanent coma as the result of a drugs overdose. She was placed on a respirator. Her parents applied to the hospital authorities to have their daughter removed from the respirator. This request was refused and the matter went to court. At the initial hearing, it was held that the patient not be removed from the respirator. On appeal to the Supreme Court of New Jersey, it was held that there existed a constitutional right to privacy which included the right of the family of a patient such as Karen Quinlan to discontinue artificial respiration.

It is arguable whether the 'substituted judgement' doctrine is entirely appropriate in the case of a patient in a permanently unconscious state who has never expressed a preference in relation to treatment withdrawal, as the surrogate cannot really base her or his decision on the presumed preferences of such a patient.[91] However, despite such criticisms, the 'substituted judgement' doctrine has become the norm in judicial decision-making on behalf of the incompetent patient in the United States.[92]

However inadequate the 'substituted judgement' standard may be in determining whether a once-competent patient should continue to receive life-sustaining medical treatment, it would seem beyond question that it is completely inappropriate in the case of the never-competent unconscious patient. The application of the 'substituted judgement' test in the case of the never-competent is comparatively rare, but when it is applied in such cases it raises questions about the validity of using legal tools for purposes for which they were not intended.[93] In this instance the 'substituted judgement' test is arguably not the standard which should be applied. In such cases it may be more logical to apply the 'best interests' standard.[94]

The major problem with the 'best interests' test is that the 'best interests' as identified by the court may not necessarily coincide with the individual patient's best interests but rather with the 'best interests' of the patient as perceived by third parties such as the medical profession and the judiciary. The judicial track record in this area tends to a certain disequilibrium in favour of professionally perceived best interests rather than the individual patient's best interests.

As long as the judiciary does indeed act as an independent arbiter in this area then one may welcome this approach. However, the fact remains that in the medico-legal field, courts have been loathe to act as a forum for independent review. They have tended to favour the accepted practice of the medical profession and have demonstrated a marked reluctance to impinge on the professional autonomy of the physician. Thus, as Teff has noted,

'Treatment in the "best interests" of the patient'
sounds like a very reassuring criterion; deceptively so,
when one appreciates that it can be satisfied by a
medical judgement which the court and even the
preponderance of expert medical opinion would have
rejected.[95]

In the Irish context, the courts are also bound to examine the
constitutional issues raised by this aspect of medical practice. On
the constitutional issues involved in such a case, Justice Lynch in
the High Court in *Re A Ward of Court* was of the view that the right
to privacy or self-determination was of greater weight in this
context than the constitutionally protected right to life in Article
40.3.1. Justice Lynch rationalized that the right to die naturally
was part of the right to life. In the Supreme Court, Chief Justice
Hamilton, while arriving at a conclusion that upheld the legality of
withdrawing treatment in such a case, came to such a conclusion by
a different route. He was of the view that a constitutional obligation to respect the life of the ward existed in this case. However,
this obligation was not absolute and may be waived in certain
exceptional circumstances. Thus, a situation such as the one before
the court where the ward's life was being sustained by what he
termed 'abnormal artificial means' fell into the category of such
exceptions.

On the other hand, Justice Denham in her judgment in the
Supreme Court decision in the case stated that while the guarantee
in the Constitution that the state would respect the right to life
was absolute, the requirement to defend and vindicate the life was
not absolute. This she inferred from the inclusion in Article
40.3.1 of the clause 'as far as practicable'. In a case such as the one
before the court, Justice Denham believed that a decision should
be taken which preserved, defended and vindicated the ward's life.
She was of the view that in respecting a person's death, one is also

respecting a person's life. Moreover, she asserted that the right to privacy encompassed the right to die naturally.

The decision in *Re A Ward of Court* provoked strong reactions from certain groups. The pro-life lobby reacted by stating that this was an unacceptable erosion of the principle of the sanctity of life. The reaction of many health-care professionals was antipathetic to the judgment.[96] Indeed, in statements issued in the wake of the Supreme Court's decision in *Re A Ward of Court*, both the Irish Medical Council and An Bord Altranis (the Irish Nursing Board) were of the view that it is not ethical for a doctor or a nurse to withdraw artificial hydration or nutrition from a patient who is not dying.[97] It would appear that the Irish Medical Council disregards the approach taken by the Supreme Court in relation to treatment withdrawal by announcing that

> It is the view of the Council that access to nutrition and hydration is one of the basic needs of human beings. This remains so even when, from time to time, this need can only be fulfilled by means of long established methods such as naso-gastric and gast-ronomy tube feeding.[98]

In the statement issued by the Medical Council in response to the Supreme Court's decision on treatment withdrawal, the Council, by quoting selectively from its *Guide to Ethical Conduct and Behaviour and to Fitness to Practise* criticized implicity the stance taken by the Supreme Court. Thus, the inclusion in the statement of the following paragraph from the ethical guidelines can only be seen as a veiled attack on the Supreme Court's decision: 'Medical care must not be used as a tool of the State to be granted or withheld or altered in character under political pressure.'[99]

This reaction was similar to the Medical Council's reaction to the Supreme Court's decision in *Attorney General v X.*[100] In the aftermath of that decision the Medical Council took an equally divergent stance by announcing that doctors who performed abortions were acting unethically.[101] Thus, the moral intransigence of the medical profession in Ireland leads to a situation where legal decisions of enormous constitutional and symbolic importance are made difficult to implement.[102]

The question thus has to be asked whether the courts, while upholding the rights of the individual, are reflecting an attitudinal shift or are provoking that shift in attitude? Are law and society in harmony on contentious social issues or does there remain in Irish society an innate social conservatism which no Supreme Court decision can penetrate?[103] The evidence would seem to indicate that Irish courts have been placed in the position of tackling controversial issues of social policy which conservative and weak coalition governments have in the past been afraid to tackle.[104] As Girvin has noted, the fact that the Supreme Court has, since the 1970s, become the forum for directing change, 'reflected the reluctance of politicians to act rather than the reality of an activist Supreme Court.'[105]

In theory, the pronouncements by the Supreme Court in cases such as *Attorney General v X* and *Re A Ward of Court*, whilst reflecting a move away from the absoluteness of the sanctity of life model on the plane of constitutional discourse, may not yet reflect the interpretation of the sanctity of life on the plane of cultural discourse. This may be gauged by looking at the reaction of health-care professionals and pro-life groups to these decisions. On this level the issues are far from resolved. There seem to exist in Ireland parallel streams of thought as to what constitutes the right to life. On the level of legal discourse, as reflected in cases like *Re A Ward of Court*, the emphasis is on the idea of patient autonomy. However, at the level of professional discourse, the emphasis continues to be placed on beneficence rather than patient autonomy.

This mirrors the wider societal dichotomy of liberal and conservative values existing side by side in an uneasy relationship. As O'Leary and Hesketh have noted,

> the Irish electorate does not fit easily into the
> deterministic strait-jackets proffered by a number of
> scholars. It is not a situation of gradual – or even for
> that matter of declining – liberalisation, but one in
> which liberal and traditional values exist side by side
> in a complex relationship . . .[106]

Behind the façade of modernizing lurks a conservatism reinforced in its resolve by the current paradigm swing.

The residual importance of the influence of the Roman Catholic Church on issues of moral controversy can be witnessed by the fact that in the High Court hearing of *Re A Ward of Court* moral theologians from the Roman Catholic Church were called to give evidence in relation to the morality of treatment withdrawal. In addition Justice Lynch received a Working Paper from the Church of Ireland detailing its view on euthanasia. Justice Lynch gave the following justification for allowing the hearing of evidence in relation to the ethics of euthanasia:

> the evidence of the moral theologians is of relevance
> for two reasons: first, as showing that in proposing the
> course which they do propose the Ward's family are
> not contravening their own ethic . . . and secondly,
> the matter being *res integra*, the views of theologians of
> various faiths are of assistance in that they endeavour
> to apply right reason to the problems for decision by
> the Court and analogous problems.[107]

Two Roman Catholic theologians were called to give evidence on behalf of the ward's family. They were both of the view that the family's desire to have treatment withdrawn was in keeping with Roman Catholic moral guidance on the issue. However, another Roman Catholic theologian who gave evidence on behalf of the institution in which the ward was being treated argued that this was not the case. This demonstrates that while there may be division within the Roman Catholic Church on the issue, the eventual decision arrived at by both the High Court and the Supreme Court in this case is not antithetical to Roman Catholic moral teaching. However, those like pro-life groups and health-care professionals who have not been acculturated into the intricacies of Roman Catholic theology have argued that such an outcome is antithetical to traditional cultural values as opposed to religious values *per se*. This is not a rigorous philosophical or theological stance, but one based on a perceived notion of traditional Irish societal values and further complicates the Irish debate on the right to die.

The medical and nursing professions in Ireland have a reputation for conservatism on issues of bioethical controversy.[108] Moreover, many hospitals are under the stewardship of Roman Catholic nursing orders, as was the case with the institution in which the patient in *Re A Ward of Court* had been treated, and would be antipathetic to treatment withdrawal for incurably ill unconscious patients. Thus, it may be argued, in reality the ability to exercise autonomy in relation to the right to die in the health-care context is constrained first and foremost by the health-care professions' conception of morality rather than by Roman Catholic dogma *per se*. This is not to say that the Roman Catholic Church does not maintain a certain influence in this area. However, today, it may be more correct to state that the notions of morality held by professional groups and lay pro-life groups have filled the vacuum left in public discourse by the diminishing role played by the institutional Church in the formulation of public policy on areas of moral controversy. Due to the barriers erected by the antithetical views of certain groups in society, the Supreme Court's activist stance has resulted in an apparent shift on the symbolic level to a less conservative model of the right to life but has led to little change in terms of being actually able to exercise one's right to die.

5. Ending Life: Active Voluntary

Euthanasia

The medical professional is generally perceived as playing the role of life-preserver, in effect, the nemesis of death. However, in one aspect of medical practice – in the care of the dying or incurably ill patient – the roles tend to be reversed and the medical practitioner becomes the pariah, seemingly abandoning Hippocratic responsibilities and siding with vengeful death.

Thus, the doctor who departs from the Hippocratic injunction, 'to please no one will I prescribe a deadly drug, nor give advice which may cause his death',[109] would seem to be departing from a fundamental tenet of the medical profession.

However, as in most medical dilemmas, the situation is not as easily resolved as this. One must look to the reasons which prompt a doctor to take such a course of action and to the wishes of the patient involved if competent or, in the case of the incompetent patient, the wishes of the next-of-kin or the previously expressed wishes of the patient when in a competent state.

Central to this issue is the way in which death and life are perceived in a given society, the perception of the role of the doctor in society and the value given to the autonomy of the individual. These values tend to be reflected in the approach of both the legislature and the judiciary to the question of inducing the death of a patient.

Active euthanasia occurs when a doctor carries out a positive act which results in the death of a patient. This may take the form of the doctor administering a lethal injection to the patient. This act may be carried out at the request of the patient, in which case it is termed 'active voluntary euthanasia'. Alternatively, the patient may not be capable of consenting to his or her death, in which case such medical intervention is termed 'non-voluntary active euthanasia'.

Moreover, one must distinguish between the term physician-assisted suicide and the term active euthanasia. This is an important, if obvious, requirement, as the two distinct concepts are often fused.[110] In the case of physician-assisted suicide, the doctor furnishes the patient with the means to terminate his or her life but does not act positively to terminate that patient's life – for example, when the doctor writes a prescription for a lethal dose of bar-biturates, or, as in the case of Dr Jack Kevorkian, when the doctor sets up a suicide machine in a patient's home, leaving the patient to carry out the act of releasing the lethal gas fumes which will bring about death. Rather, it is the patients who bring about death by purchasing those pills and ingesting them or by inducing the emission of lethal gas. Active euthanasia involves the doctor in supplying the means of death and acting as the agent who brings about the patient's death, as, for example, in the case of a doctor who administers a lethal dose of a pain-killing injection to a patient who has given valid consent. Quill, Cassel and Meier have pointed out the more democratic nature of the former method as a means of giving legal validity to a right to die:

> the balance of power between doctor and patient is more nearly equal in physician-assisted suicide than in euthanasia. The physician is counsellor and witness and makes the means available, but ultimately the patient must be the one to act or not. In voluntary euthanasia, the physician both provides the means and carries out the final act, with greatly amplified power over the patient and an increased risk of error, coercion or abuse.[111]

This approach neatly counters the twin pillars of the traditional anti-euthanasia argument, namely, the slippery slope and abuse arguments, and respects both the individual autonomy of the patient and the doctor's professional integrity. Perhaps it is this model that Irish legislators should consider when the hoary old issue of euthanasia comes onto the constitutional and policy agenda – an ineluctable occurrence given both demographic and health-policy trends. It is, therefore, appropriate to examine the varying legal models which would give legal effect to the act of physician-assisted suicide.

Neither active euthanasia nor physician-assisted suicide are deemed lawful in Ireland. Thus, a doctor who gives a patient a lethal dose of a drug with the intention of accelerating the patient's end would arguably be charged with murder. There have been no Irish cases specifically on this issue nor does there exist specific legislation on the point. However, it was pointed out in passing by the Chief Justice in his decision in *Re A Ward of Court*[112] that 'It is important to emphasise that the court can never sanction steps to terminate life . . . any course of action or treatment aimed at terminating life or accelerating death is unlawful.'[113]

Moreover, the practice of assisted suicide is prohibited by section 2(2) of the *Criminal Law (Suicide) Act* 1993 which states that

> A person who aids, abets, counsels or procures the suicide of another, or an attempt by another to commit suicide, shall be guilty of an offence and shall be liable on conviction on indictment to imprisonment for a term not exceeding fourteen years.

Thus, the physician in Ireland who felt compelled to assist a patient's suicide would satisfy the requirements for such an offence.

However, the question must be asked, as it has been, for example, in the United States, whether one could successfully argue that the prohibition of physician-assisted suicide violated an individual's constitutional rights, particularly the right to privacy and the right to equal treatment. A major argument against such a development would be the killing and letting die distinction as understood by the criminal law. A proponent of such a distinction in the Irish context is Justice Costello who has engaged in the casuistical exercise of distinguishing between active and passive means of euthanasia.[114] In the course of his argument he explicitly ruled out the legality of assisted suicide.[115]

Nonetheless, it may be of value to analyse decisions in this area in other jurisdictions that have attempted to tackle the problem with a view to outlining solutions other than the traditional Irish one of ignoring the issue.

CONSTITUTIONAL ARGUMENTS

Washington is one of almost twenty-five US states which provide for the introduction of legislation by direct vote on an initiative petition. In 1991 the Hemlock Society put forward an initiative petition relating to physician-assisted suicide. Initiative 119, as it was called, provided for what was termed 'physician aid in dying' by means of an amendment to Washington's Natural Death Act 1979.[116] The framers of the initiative defined the term 'physician aid in dying' as

> a medical service, provided in person by a physician, that will end the life of a conscious and mentally com-petent qualified patient in a dignified, painless and humane manner, when requested voluntarily by the patient through a written directive.[117]

The difficulty with such wording was that it did not distinguish adequately between the practice of physician-assisted suicide and the practice of active euthanasia. The voters were, as a result, unsure of the exact nature of the practice for which they were voting, and were easily swayed by the hyperbole of anti-euthanasia campaigners. The initiative was defeated with 54 per cent of those who voted voting against the initiative, and 46 per cent voting for the initiative.

As a result of this experience a pressure group, Compassion in Dying, which provides support and counselling for mentally competent, terminally ill adults considering suicide, initiated a legal challenge to Washington's law prohibiting physician-assisted suicide in the case of terminally ill persons.[118] This law provides that those who assist another to commit suicide shall be guilty of a felony. This offence is punishable by imprisonment for a maximum of five years and a fine of up to $10,000.

The pressure group was joined in the action by three terminally ill patients and four physicians who are involved in the care of the terminally ill. The three patients wanted to be enabled to obtain prescriptions for lethal doses of drugs from their doctors, arguing that they had a constitutionally protected interest guaranteed by the Fourteenth Amendment to the Constitution to commit suicide with the aid of a doctor. The physicians also alleged that the Fourteenth Amendment protects their right to practise medicine consistent with their best professional judgement, including the right to assist competent, terminally ill adult patients to hasten death, by prescribing suitable medication for self-administration by the patient. Compassion in Dying, for its part, claimed that competent, terminally ill adults have the right to request assistance from its staff members, which would include both counselling and the delivering or mixing of the drugs to be used.

Lawyers on behalf of the state argued that laws outlawing assisted suicide were required in order to protect vulnerable members of society who, through undue influence, may be persuaded to commit suicide. Moreover, the state argued, if the practice of physician-assisted suicide were to be legalized, those other than the terminally ill may be persuaded to avail of it, another variant on the slippery slope argument.

It was held by the Washington Federal District Court judge that the statute was unconstitutional, as it denied equal protection under the law to competent terminally ill patients who had no life-sustaining treatment to refuse. This was due to the provisions in Washington's Natural Death Act 1979 which allowed terminally ill patients to use advance directives to order the withholding or withdrawal of treatment in the case of terminal illness or in the case of their entering a state of permanent unconsciousness. This could be seen as treating different classes of persons in an unequal manner.

In speaking of the constitutionally protected liberty interest, Judge Rothstein referred to previous Supreme Court jurisprudence on the issue. In particular, she referred to the case of *Planned Parenthood v Casey*.[119] In *Planned Parenthood v Casey* the liberty interest involved was a woman's right to choose abortion. Judge Rothstein, while stating that the decision in *Planned Parenthood v Casey* was different in substance from the instant case, found the reasoning in that case to be of particular relevance. She stated that even though *Planned Parenthood v Casey*

> involved a woman's right to choose abortion, and thus did not address the question of what liberty interest may inhere in a terminally ill person's choice to commit suicide . . . this court finds the reasoning in *Casey* highly instructive and almost prescriptive on the latter issue. Like the abortion decision, the decision of a terminally ill person to end his or her life 'involves the most intimate and personal choices a person may make in a lifetime' and constitutes a 'choice central to personal dignity and autonomy'.[120]

The judge then compared the issues of abortion and physician-assisted suicide in terms of the moral divisiveness engendered by both issues. She stressed the need to avoid imposing moral stand-

ards on such issues in the place of legal analysis. She cited the
following passage from *Planned Parenthood v Casey* as a basis for her
analysis of the issue:

> Our obligation is to define the liberty of all, not
> to mandate our own moral code. The underlying con-
> stitutional issue is whether the State can resolve these
> philosophic questions in such a definitive way that a
> woman lacks all choice in the matter.[121]

In applying the reasoning in *Planned Parenthood v Casey* to the
instant case, Judge Rothstein was of the opinion that

> the suffering of a terminally ill person cannot be deemed
> any less intimate or personal, or any less deserving of
> protection from unwarranted governmental interfer-
> ence, than that of a pregnant woman. Thus, consonant
> with the reasoning in *Casey*, such an intimate personal
> decision falls within the realm of the liberties constitu-
> tionally protected under the Fourteenth Amendment.[122]

Judge Rothstein also adverted to the Supreme Court decision in
Cruzan v Director, Missouri Department of Health[123] in her judgment.
Cruzan v Director, Missouri Department of Health was concerned with
the related but distinct issue of refusal of life-sustaining medical
treatment. In *Cruzan v Director, Missouri Department of Health* the
Supreme Court was of the opinion that a competent person has a
constitutionally protected right to refuse artificial hydration and
nutrition. Judge Rothstein in the instant case was confident that

> squarely faced with the issue, the Supreme Court
> would reaffirm Rehnquist J.'s tentative conclusion in
> *Cruzan* that a competent person has a protected liberty
> interest in refusing unwanted medical treatment, even

when that treatment is life-sustaining and refusal or withdrawal of the treatment would mean certain death. The question then becomes whether a constitutional distinction can be drawn between refusal or withdrawal of medical treatment which results in death, and the situation in this case involving competent, terminally ill individuals who wish to hasten death by self-administering drugs prescribed by a physician.[124]

Judge Rothstein was of the opinion that there was no appreciable difference between the liberty interest protected in both instances. She stated that the liberty interest protected by the Fourteenth Amendment

is the freedom to make choices according to one's individual conscience about those matters which are essential to personal autonomy and basic human dignity. There is no more profoundly personal decision, nor one which is closer to the heart of personal liberty, than the choice which a terminally ill person makes to end his or her suffering and hasten an inevitable death. From a constitutional perspective, the court does not believe that a distinction can be drawn between refusing life-sustaining medical treatment and physician-assisted suicide by an uncoerced, mentally competent, terminally ill adult.[125]

On the question of equal protection, Judge Rothstein supported the plaintiffs' contention that the statute in question violated the Equal Protection Clause of the Fourteenth Amendment. The Equal Protection Clause provides that all those who are similarly situated should be treated alike. When a state law is found to violate the constitutionally protected rights of certain individuals but not of others in a similar situation then such a law may be subjected to what is termed 'strict scrutiny' and will only be upheld if it can be demonstrated that such a state of affairs serves a compelling state interest.[126]

In this case, the two similarly situated groups were, on the one hand, mentally competent, terminally ill adults whose condition involves the use of life-sustaining equipment and who may lawfully obtain medical assistance in terminating such treatment and, on the other hand, mentally competent, terminally ill adults whose treatment does not involve the use of life-support systems and who are denied the opportunity of hastening death with medical assistance.

On the point of the unequal treatment afforded both groups, the judge recognized the governmental interest in preventing suicide as being a compelling state interest, but observed that both the Washington Natural Death Act 1979 and Washington case-law had created an exception for terminally ill patients and those in a permanent unconscious state wishing to terminate life-support.[127]

Judge Rothstein was thus of the view that the state had already recognized that its interest in preventing suicide did not require an absolute ban. She went on to state that

> Washington law, by creating an exception for those patients on life support, yet not permitting competent, terminally ill adult patients such as plaintiffs the equivalent option of exercising their rights to hasten their deaths with medical assistance, creates a situation in which the fundamental rights of one group are burdened while those of a similarly situated group are not. Therefore, this court finds that [the Washington statute forbidding assisted suicide] violates the equal protection guarantee of the Fourteenth Amendment.[128]

As regards the standard of review to be applied in the case, Judge Rothstein was of the opinion that the standard laid down in

Planned Parenthood v Casey should be applicable. In *Planned P*
v Casey the Supreme Court held that, in order to demonst
unconstitutionality of a state statute, the plaintiffs had to sh
it would operate as a substantial obstacle to the exercis
constitutional right, and would, as a result, constitute an
burden.[129] In applying this standard to the case, Judge Rotl
first looked at the interests of the state in upholding the statu

The interests were twofold. Firstly, the statute purporte
further the interest of preventing suicide, and, secondly, it purpo
to protect those at risk of suicide from undue influence fr
others who would aid them in that act. In answer to the fi
contention, it was held that

> The state's interest in preventing suicide by prohibiting
> any manner of assisted suicide in actuality arises out of
> its apprehension of the 'slippery slope' problem. The
> State is concerned that allowing any exception to a
> total ban will encourage the gradual development of a
> more permissive attitude toward suicide . . . However,
> that is not a sufficient excuse for precluding entirely
> the exercise of a constitutional right. The court has no
> doubt that the legislature can devise regulations which
> will define the appropriate boundaries of physician-
> assisted suicide for terminally ill individuals, and at the
> same time give due recognition to the important public
> policy concerns regarding the prevention of suicide.[130]

In relation to the state's contention pertaining to undue
influence and duress in assisted suicide cases, it was held that

> it is undisputed that plaintiffs in this case are mentally
> competent individuals who have reached a decision to
> commit physician-assisted suicide free of any undue
> influence. Thus, the plaintiffs and others who make

knowing and voluntary choices to commit physician-assisted suicide by definition fall outside the realm of the State's concern.[131]

Moreover, the judge observed that Washington law already permitted an individual to refuse life-sustaining treatment in the event of terminal illness or entering a state of permanent unconsciousness. In those cases, the judge pointed out, the potential risk of abuse was also present. Judge Rothstein concluded that it would be possible for the legislature to

> devise regulations which would set up a mechanism for ensuring that people who decide to commit physician-assisted suicide are not acting pursuant to abuse, coercion or undue influence from third parties.[132]

On appeal a three-judge panel of the United States Court of Appeals for the Ninth Circuit voted by a two-to-one majority to reverse the decision of the Washington Federal District Court.[133] It was then decided, due to the enormous importance of the case, that it be reheard *en banc* (i.e. in front of a full panel of the Ninth Circuit Court of Appeals, consisting of eleven judges). It was held at this hearing that insofar as the Washington statute in question prohibits physicians from prescribing life-ending medication for use by terminally ill, competent adults who wish to hasten their own deaths, it violated the Due Process Clause of the Fourteenth Amendment to the Constitution of the United States. This case is currently under appeal to the Supreme Court of the United States.

In a 1991 article, Dr Timothy Quill, a New York oncologist, related how he had assisted a patient to commit suicide.[134] The patient was terminally ill and wished to hasten her death to prevent further suffering. After discussing the matter with her family and agreeing to meet with Dr Quill prior to taking an overdose of

barbiturates, the doctor agreed to write a prescription for barbiturates. She eventually arrived at a point where she wished to end her life. She discussed the matter with her family and with Dr Quill, after which she took an overdose of barbiturates and died. As a result of this 'confession' Dr Quill became the subject of a criminal investigation.

This resulted from the fact that assisted suicide is deemed to be a felony in New York. Section 125.15(3) of the New York Penal Law 1881 provides that a person shall be guilty of manslaughter in the second degree if he or she intentionally aids another person to commit suicide. In addition, section 120.30 provides that a person shall be guilty of promoting a suicide attempt when he or she intentionally aids another person to attempt suicide. Dr Quill was obliged to appear before a grand jury but the grand jury did not indict.

Subsequently, Dr Quill attempted to seek a preliminary injunction in a New York District Court against the enforcement of sections 125.15(3) and 120.30 of the New York Penal Law 1881 to the extent that they apply to physicians who give the kind of assistance that Dr Quill gave to his patient.[135] This was based on the argument that such statutory provisions violated the rights of the terminally ill and physicians under the Due Process and Equal Protection Clauses of the Fourteenth Amendment to the Constitution. The New York District Court did not accept this argument and refused to grant the preliminary injunction.

This decision was subsequently appealed to the United States Court of Appeals for the Second Circuit.[136] The Court of Appeals for the Second Circuit reversed the previous decision in part, holding that physicians who are willing to do so may prescribe drugs to be self-administered by mentally competent patients who seek to end their lives during the final stages of a terminal illness. The Court of Appeals accepted the plaintiffs' argument based on the Equal Protection Clause of the Fourteenth Amendment to the Constitution of the United States. According to the Fourteenth

Amendment, the equal protection of the laws cannot be denied by any state to any person within its jurisdiction. The Equal Protection Clause requires the individual states to treat in a similar way all individuals who are similarly situated. Applying the Equal Protection Clause to the New York legislation which the plaintiffs challenged, the Court of Appeals was of the view that the statutes in question did not treat equally all competent persons who are in the final stages of a fatal illness and who wish to hasten their deaths. The distinctions made by New York law with regard to such persons did not, according to the court, further any legitimate state interest and accordingly, to the extent that the statutes in question prohibited persons in the final stages of a terminal illness from having assistance in ending their lives by the use of self-administered, prescribed drugs, the statutes lacked any rational basis and were in violation of the Equal Protection Clause. Thus, New York law allowed those individuals in the final stages of a terminal illness who are on life-support systems to hasten their deaths by directing the removal of such systems, but it did not allow those who were similarly situated, except for the fact that they were not attached to a life-support system, to hasten death by self-administering prescribed drugs.

The Court of Appeals referred to the chimeric nature of the act—omission argument in this context:

> there is nothing 'natural' about causing death by means other than the original illness or its complications. The withdrawal of nutrition brings on death by starvation, the removal of hydration brings on death by dehydration, and the withdrawal of ventilation brings about respiratory failure. By ordering the discontinuance of these artificial, life-sustaining processes or refusing to accept them in the first place, a patient hastens his death by means that are not natural in any sense. It

certainly cannot be said that the death that immediately ensues is the natural result of the progression of the disease or condition from which the patient suffers.

Moreover, the writing of a prescription to hasten death, after consultation with a patient, involves a far less active role for the physician than is required in bringing about death through asphyxiation, starvation and/or dehydration. Withdrawal of life support requires physicians or those acting at their direction physically to remove equipment and, often, to administer palliative drugs which may themselves contribute to death. The ending of life by these means is nothing more nor less than assisted suicide. It simply cannot be said that those mentally competent, terminally ill persons who seek to hasten death but whose treatment does not include life support are treated equally.[137]

Because of the enormous constitutional importance of the issues raised by this case, the Supreme Court of the United States has agreed to review the case in its current term. A decision of the Supreme Court on the issue of physician-assisted suicide is expected by July 1997.

The court will be faced with the different decisions of the Ninth Circuit Court of Appeals and the Second Circuit Court of Appeals. Both courts held that statutes outlawing assisted suicide were unconstitutional but for different reasons. The Ninth Circuit justified its decision on the basis that the Washington statute was contrary to the Due Process Clause of the Fourteenth Amendment, while the Second Circuit Court of Appeals held that New York state legislation rendering assisted suicide unlawful was unconstitutional in that it was contrary to the Equal Protection Clause of the Fourteenth Amendment.

In Canada, the right to physician-assisted suicide is impeded by the presence in the Canadian Criminal Code 1892 of section

241(b) which prohibits the aiding and abetting of suicide. Section 241 provides that anyone who counsels, aids or abets another to commit suicide shall be guilty of an indictable offence and is liable to imprisonment for a term not exceeding fourteen years. This provision is similar to the provision to be found in section 2(2) of the Irish Criminal Law (Suicide) Act 1993, which provides that any person who aids, abets, counsels or procures the suicide of another shall be liable on conviction on indictment for a term not exceeding fourteen years.

It is interesting therefore to examine the law in relation to physician-assisted suicide in Canada, a country with a comparable common-law and constitutional tradition to Ireland, with a view to predicting the likely alternatives open to the Irish judiciary and legislature in this area. In 1982, the Law Reform Commission of Canada tried to rationalize the presence of the section 241 pro-hibition on aiding suicide in the following terms:

> What of the person who takes advantage of another's depressed state to encourage him to commit suicide, for his own financial benefit? What of the person who, knowing an adolescent's suicidal tendencies, provides him with large enough quantities of drugs to kill him? The 'accomplice' in these cases cannot be morally blameless. Nor can one conclude that the criminal law should not punish such conduct. To decriminalize com-pletely the act of aiding, abetting or counselling suicide would therefore not be a valid legislative policy.[138]

The Commission went on to consider the question of assisted suicide for the terminally ill:

> The probable reason why legislation has not made an exception for the terminally ill is the fear of the excesses or abuses to which liberalization of the existing

law could lead. As in the case of 'compassionate murder', decriminalization of aiding suicide would be based on the humanitarian nature of the motive leading the person to provide such aid, counsel or encouragement. As in the case of compassionate murder, moreover, the law may legitimately fear the difficulties involved in determining the true motivation of the person committing the act.

Aiding or counselling a person to commit suicide, on the one hand, and homicide, on the other, are sometimes extremely closely related. Consider, for example, the doctor who holds the glass of poison and pours the contents into the patient's mouth. Is he aiding him to commit suicide? Or is he committing homicide, since the victim's willingness to die is legally immaterial? There is reason to fear that homicide of the terminally ill for ignoble motives may readily be disguised as aiding suicide.[139]

In the report[140] which followed the Working Paper, the Law Reform Commission rejected the idea of decriminalizing or legalizing active voluntary euthanasia.

The aforementioned provisions of the Criminal Code were later to be challenged on constitutional grounds in the case of *Re Rodriguez and Attorney General of British Columbia et al.; British Columbia Coalition of People with Disabilities et al.; Interveners*.[141] In this case the appellant was a forty-two-year-old woman who suffered from Lou Gehrig's Disease.[142]

The appellant, knowing of the prognosis, had expressed a wish to die, when, as a result of the disease, the quality of her life deteriorated substantially. At that point, she would be unable to end her own life and would require the assistance of a medical practitioner to do so. Mrs Rodriguez, therefore, applied to the Supreme Court of British Columbia for an order stating that section 241(b) of the Criminal Code 1892 be declared invalid, pursuant to section 24(1) of the Canadian Charter of Rights and Freedoms 1982, on the basis that it violated the rights enunciated in sections 7, 12 and 15(1) of the Canadian Charter of Rights and Freedoms 1982.[143]

The Supreme Court of British Columbia refused to grant the order sought by the appellant. The trial judge believed that to interpret section 7 of the Canadian Charter of Rights and Freedoms 1982 so as to include a constitutionally guaranteed right to take one's own life as an exercise in freedom of choice was inconsistent with the right to life, liberty and the security of the person. The argument based on section 12 of the Canadian Charter of Rights and Freedoms 1982 was rejected on the grounds that it was the illness from which the appellant suffered, and not the state justice system, which had prevented her from determining the time and manner of her death. The appellant also argued that because it is not unlawful to refuse life-saving or life-prolonging medical treatment, or to commit suicide, or to accelerate death through therapeutic doses of pain-relievers, to make physician-assisted suicide unlawful discriminates against physically disabled people. This argument was also rejected. The decision was appealed to the British Columbia Court of Appeals, which dismissed the appeal by a majority of two-to-one.

The Court of Appeals was of the opinion that the proper forum to address a matter of such moral and social complexity was parliament. In the words of Justice Proudfoot for the majority,

> the broad religious, ethical, moral and social issues implicit in the merits of this case are not suited to resolution by a court on affidavit evidence at the instance of a single individual. On the material available to us, we are in no position to assess the consensus in Canada with respect to assisted suicide . . . I would

leave to Parliament the responsibility of taking the pulse of the nation.[144]

The appellant, as a result, decided to appeal the decision to the Canadian Supreme Court. The appeal was dismissed by a majority of five-to-four in the Supreme Court. The majority was of the opinion that, despite section 241(b) of the Criminal Code 1892 having the effect of interfering with the appellant's autonomy over her person, causing her physical pain and psychological stress in a manner which impinged on the security of her person, it was neither arbitrary nor unfair and was grounded in the state interest in protecting life.

Thus, respect for the sanctity of life was the justification for limiting personal autonomy in this instance. In the words of Justice Sopinka for the majority,

> To the extent that there is a consensus, it is that human life must be respected and we must be careful not to undermine the institutions that protect it.
>
> This consensus finds legal expression in our legal system which prohibits capital punishment. This prohibition is supported, in part, on the basis that allowing the state to kill will cheapen the value of human life and thus the state will serve in a sense as a role model for individuals in society. The prohibition against assisted suicide serves a similar purpose. In upholding the respect for life, it may discourage those who consider that life is unbearable at a particular moment, or who perceive themselves to be a burden upon others, from committing suicide. To permit a physician to lawfully participate in taking life would send a signal that there are circumstances in which the state approves of suicide . . .
>
> Given the concerns about abuse that have been expressed and the great difficulty in creating appropriate

safeguards to prevent these, it cannot be said that the blanket prohibition on assisted suicide is arbitrary or unfair, or that it is not reflective of fundamental values at play in our society. I am thus unable to find that any principle of fundamental justice is violated by section 241(b).[145]

Despite this defence of the value which is to be placed on life as a moral good, the Supreme Court did not appear to object to the practice of treatment withdrawal or passive euthanasia, which is legally permissible in Canada.[146] Justice Sopinka for the majority provided the following rationale for the differential treatment of active intervention to end life and treatment withdrawal:

> Whether or not one agrees that the active versus passive distinction is maintainable, however, the fact remains that under our common law, the physician has no choice but to accept the patient's instructions to discontinue treatment. To continue to treat the patient when the patient has withdrawn consent to that treatment constitutes battery . . . The doctor is, therefore, not required to make a choice which will result in the patient's death as he would if he chose to assist a suicide or to perform active euthanasia.[147]

However, is this sufficient justification for restricting the autonomy of the patient who wishes to die by active means? It could be argued that the legislative and judicial framework which is imposed on the relationship between individual actors in such a situation is yet another example of legal rhetoric restricting individual rights. Is not the law in relation to murder but a social and cultural construct which merely reflects a particular idea of social reality and organization? Such a view is manifest in the classical theory of natural law. This deontological view sees acts as being either good or evil in a very general sense regardless of the surrounding circumstances and the motivations of the individual actors.

Thus, killing is deemed to be wrong except in certain specified circumstances, such as, for example, in time of war or in the case of capital punishment. Applying this model to the particular fact situation of taking life, the act is looked at in an entirely objective sense, that is, *A* acts with the intention of bringing about *B*'s death and in fact brings about the death of *B*. This is killing, and killing is wrong. The surrounding circumstances of the case are not examined. *A* may represent a bank robber who kills *B*, a bank assistant, in the course of a robbery or *A* may be a doctor who wants to ease the suffering of *B*, a cancer-ridden patient who consents to this intervention. Is the criminal law too blunt an instrument to be used in such cases? As Silving has noted,

> the use of legal technicalities in [the] acquittal of [mercy-killers] tends to give laymen the impression that the law is a magic formula rather than an honest tool for meting out justice. Public confidence in the administration of criminal justice is hardly strengthened when moral issues are shifted instead of being solved, or when the law relegates to juries the function of correcting its inequities.[148]

Thus, the legal fiction of creating a legally significant difference between acts of commission and acts of omission places a barrier in the way of justice rather than contributing towards a system of criminal justice which is fair to all. In this instance, the rules of the criminal law tend to cause injustice in the sense of unfairness, in that the doctor who actively intervenes to ease the suffering of the patient with the patient's consent is deemed to be both morally and legally culpable whereas the doctor who indirectly brings about the death of the patient through, for example, the disconnecting of a life-support machine is not treated similarly under the rhetoric of criminal justice. How is one to square this anomaly with the aspiration of equal justice for all?

Moreover, the autonomy of the patient who voluntarily requests that the doctor administer a lethal dose of a drug is not respected. Thus, Sue Rodriguez, who was unable to end her own suffering due to the physical barrier caused by her illness, was to be denied her right to decide her own fate. In the words of Steven Wolhandler,

> It is legally inconsistent to honour a terminal patient's request that life support equipment be removed, but to deny a similarly situated patient's request for an immediate and painless end merely because a second party's active assistance is needed to implement the latter request. Prohibiting a second party from helping a patient commit self-euthanasia by imposing legal sanctions on that party is effectively equivalent to denying the patient the right to make that decision in the first place.[149]

Chief Justice Lamer in his dissenting judgment emphasized the discriminatory element of legislation which prevented a certain class of persons from exercising their autonomy. He believed that section 241(b) of the Criminal Code 1892 was repugnant to the equality provisions contained in section 15(1) of the Canadian Charter of Rights and Freedoms 1982. The Chief Justice stated that section 241(b) of the Criminal Code 1892 infringes the principle of equality, in that it prevents those who are physically disabled from choosing suicide, when that option is in principle available to other members of the public. This inequality is imposed on persons unable to end their lives unassisted, solely because of a physical disability, a personal characteristic which is one of the grounds of discrimination listed in section 15(1) of the Canadian Charter of Rights and Freedoms 1982.

In Ireland it is possible to argue since the Supreme Court's decision in the case of *Re A Ward of Court* that the criminalization of physician-assisted suicide is contrary to the equality provisions of the Constitution. This argument could take a similar approach to the one made by the applicant in the *Rodriguez* case. Given the cautious manner in which both the courts and the legislature operate in the area of issues affecting the sanctity of life, it is submitted that the Irish Supreme Court would, if presented with such a case as that of Sue Rodriguez, adopt a similar position to that of the majority in that case. As for the argument based on the right of privacy, the assumption is that the Irish Supreme Court would not depart radically from its previous decisions in this area by declaring that there is a right to die by assistance. Such a radical departure would not be in accord with the way in which the right to life is currently conceptualized in Irish constitutional discourse. The reluctance of the Supreme Court to erode the value of life coupled with the act–omission argument would seem to preclude such a development. Moreover, the impact of such a move would affect the extant criminal legislation in relation to assisted suicide which, again for policy reasons, the Supreme Court would be loath to do.

ALTERNATIVE POLICIES

The law governing active voluntary euthanasia in the Netherlands has recently been amended to allow doctors in clearly defined circumstances to act to end the life of a terminally ill patient without suffering the full rigour of the criminal law.[150] The new regulations provide that doctors who carry out active euthanasia after the patient has requested it, or do so without the request of the patient, should report the fact to the local coroner, who in turn will inform the district attorney. The district attorney will not proceed further with the matter if it can be shown that the doctor acted within the guidelines laid down by the Justice Ministry protocols on the issue of euthanasia.[151] The practice of active voluntary euthanasia is not thereby legalized but the legislation, in effect, gives explicit legislative recognition to such a practice. This change in policy came about as a result of a growing debate on the topic of euthanasia within both medical and legal circles in the previous two decades. The importance of this debate was recognized when, in 1990, the Dutch government established a committee under the chair of Professor Remmelink, Procurator-General of the Dutch Supreme Court, which was to report in 1991.[152]

Article 293 of the Dutch Penal Code 1891 provides that it shall be an offence to kill another at that other's request. This offence is punishable upon successful prosecution by imprisonment for a maximum period of twelve years or by a fine. This particular criminal offence covers the act of active voluntary euthanasia. In addition, Article 294 of the Penal Code 1891 provides that any person who assists in the suicide of another shall be guilty of an offence and liable to up to three years' imprisonment or to a fine. Thus, the concept of physician-assisted suicide is, in theory, deemed a criminal offence.

However, in practice, a defence was afforded to those who were charged with such offences. In the 1984 Supreme Court decision in the case of *Office of Public Prosecutions v Leendert*,[153] a doctor, who had ended the life of a terminally ill, elderly patient, successfully pleaded the defence of necessity.[154] The Supreme Court judgment noted that the following considerations should be taken into account when deciding the guilt or otherwise of the accused in such cases:

> whether and to what extent according to professional medical judgment an increasing disfigurement of the patient's personality and/or further deterioration of her already unbearable suffering were to be expected;

whether it could be expected that soon she would no
longer be able to die with dignity under circumstances
worthy of a human being; whether there were still
opportunities to alleviate her suffering.[155]

The Supreme Court referred the matter back to the Court of
Appeal, requiring that the latter determine, on the facts of the
case, whether the act of the accused in terminating the patient's
life could be construed 'from an objective medical perspective' as
'an action justified in a situation of necessity'.[156]

The Court of Appeal answered in the affirmative, and the
accused was acquitted. The Court of Appeal did, however, alter
slightly the terms of the question posed by the Supreme Court by
replacing the word 'objective' with the word 'reasonable'. Thus, the
criterion used to determine whether the act fell within the scope of
the necessity defence was whether it could be justified when meas-
ured against the standards of reasonable medical opinion.

The courts were enabled to give further guidance on the issue
of active voluntary euthanasia soon after the decision in the case of
Office of Public Prosecutions v Leendert. Keown[157] adverts to a case
involving the prosecution of a doctor, who terminated the life of
an elderly neighbour who suffered from chronic multiple sclerosis,
after receiving many requests from the latter to do so. The
Supreme Court ruled that the lower courts had failed to consider
a number of defences in convicting the accused. These defences
were: firstly, that the doctor had acted as a result of the extreme
distress of the patient, and secondly, that as a result of witnessing
this distress and suffering on the part of the patient, the doctor
herself found that she was under duress and could not act in a
manner which differed from the manner in which she had acted.

The Supreme Court referred to this state of affairs as 'acting
out of psychological necessity'. The case was referred back to the
Court of Appeal for further determination of the issues. The Court

of Appeal in this case convicted the doctor. Perhaps the reasons for this decision may be seen in the factual differences in this case. Firstly, the victim in this case was not actually a patient of the accused. This brought the relationship outside the realm of the normal doctor–patient relationship. Secondly, the accused acted independently, without seeking further medical opinion.[158]

In the case of *Office of Public Prosecutions v Chabot*,[159] Dr Chabot had assisted in the suicide of a healthy and competent woman who had expressed her wish to die since the tragic deaths of her two sons. The offence under article 294 of the Penal Code 1891 covered this act of physician-assisted suicide. However, the Supreme Court was satisfied that the accused had, in so acting, followed the guidelines laid down by the Royal Dutch Medical Association. The Supreme Court was of the opinion that Dr Chabot had established that his patient was competent to decide, was suffering unbearably, and had a voluntary, considered and long-standing wish to die. In addition, it was adduced that he had consulted fellow practitioners about the case and had also advised his patient of other options that were open to her.

However, the Supreme Court did not accept that Dr Chabot had acted in an emergency and was thereby not afforded a defence under Article 40 of the Penal Code 1891, and the accused was, as a result, found guilty. This was due to the fact that the practitioners whom the accused consulted did not see and examine the patient. Notwithstanding the fact that the accused was found guilty, the Supreme Court declined to punish him, due to the personality of the accused, as well as the circumstances in which the act took place.

Following this decision of the Supreme Court, it may now be stated that, in addition to physical suffering, psychological suffering may form the basis of a patient's request to terminate his or her life. In addition, the Supreme Court has made it clear that those requesting euthanasia do not necessarily have to be suffering from a terminal illness and that doctors who give second opinions in such cases must first examine the patient in question.

This judicial recognition of the practice of euthanasia echoed the custom of the medical profession itself in relation to the issue of active euthanasia. The Royal Dutch Medical Association had in the decade prior to the judicial pronouncements on the issue articulated a stance on the issue, stating that while the offence enunciated in the Penal Code 1891 should remain operative, there should be some form of defence or immunity from prosecution for the doctor who ended the life of an incurable patient at the latter's request.[160]

As a result of the judicial developments in this field, the Royal Dutch Medical Association established firm guidelines on the issue.[161] The *Guidelines for Euthanasia* set out the criteria required to be fulfilled so that a doctor may be afforded a defence having euthanized a patient. Firstly, the request to have one's life terminated must come freely and voluntarily from the patient. Secondly, the request must come from a patient who has based such a request solely on a fully informed knowledge of his or her condition and that such a request is based solely on the wish to end the suffering caused to the patient by that condition and not on peripheral issues such as being a burden on one's family. Thirdly, the decision to die must not be based on a temporary whim or depression but must be a continuing wish on the patient's part. Fourthly, the patient must experience his or her suffering as persistent, unbearable and hopeless. Fifthly, the doctor must consult with other medical practitioners before terminating a patient's life.

The procedures for reporting cases of active voluntary euthanasia were set out in a protocol issued by the Justice Ministry in 1990.[162] Under the protocol, medical practitioners were obliged to inform the coroner of all cases of active voluntary euthanasia. In addition, procedures for the conduct of investigations into such deaths were outlined. The protocol directed that prosecutors on receipt of the coroner's report should instigate a police investigation only if they were satisfied in the light of the facts of the case that the required guidelines had not been followed.

Thus, the crime of killing another at that other's request remains on the Dutch statute books, but those doctors who adhere to the procedures to be followed in the case of medical euthanasia shall be afforded a defence against prosecution.

In 1996, the Northern Territory in Australia became the first jurisdiction in the world to pass legislation which provided specifically for active voluntary euthanasia. However, this piece of legislation remained in operation for only six months. It was overruled by the Australian parliament in March 1997. It is nonetheless of interest to examine the provisions of this piece of legislation with a view to discovering whether legislative resolution of this contentious issue is possible. The Rights of the Terminally Ill Act 1995 allowed a terminally ill person to request the assistance of a medically qualified person to voluntarily terminate his or her life in a humane manner without such a medical professional being subjected to legal sanctions. The Act defined 'terminal illness' as

> an illness which, in reasonable medical judgment will, in the normal course, without the application of extraordinary measures or of treatment unacceptable to the patient, result in the death of the patient. [163]

For the purposes of the Act, section 3 defined the term 'illness' broadly as including 'injury or degeneration of mental or physical faculties'.

Section 4 of the Act dealt with the manner in which one may request to have one's life ended by assistance. It provided that

> A patient who, in the course of a terminal illness, is experiencing pain, suffering and/or distress to an extent unacceptable to the patient, may request the patient's medical practitioner to assist the patient to terminate the patient's life.

A medical practitioner who received a request of this nature, if satisfied that the conditions set out in section 7 of the Act have been met and subject to the stipulations in section 8 of the Act, could then assist in terminating the patient's life in accordance with the provisions of the Act. Section 7 set out the conditions under which medical practitioners could assist a terminally ill patient to die:

(a) the patient must be at least eighteen years of age;

(b) the medical practitioner must be satisfied that:

    (i) the patient is suffering from an illness that will, in the normal course and without the application of extra-ordinary measures, result in the death of the patient;

    (ii) in reasonable medical judgment, there is no medical measure acceptable to the patient that can be reasonably undertaken in the hope of effecting a cure; and

    (iii) any medical treatment reasonably available to the patient is confined to the relief of pain, suffering and/or distress with the object of allowing the patient to die a comfortable death;

(c) two other persons, neither of whom is a relative or employee of, or a member of the same medical practice as, the first medical practitioner or each other

    (i) one of whom is a medical practitioner who holds prescribed qualifications, or has prescribed experience, in the treatment of the terminal illness from which the patient is suffering; and

    (ii) the other is a qualified psychiatrist, have examined the patient and have

    (iii) in the case of the medical practitioner, confirmed

        (A) the first medical practitioner's opinion as to the existence and seriousness of the illness;

        (B) that the patient is likely to die as a result of the illness; and

        (C) the first medical practitioner's prognosis; and

(iv) in the case of the qualified psychiatrist, that the patient is not suffering from a treatable clinical depression in respect of the illness;

(d) the illness is causing the patient severe pain or suffering;

(e) the medical practitioner has informed the patient of the nature of the illness and its likely course, and the medical treatment, including palliative care, counselling and psychiatric support and extraordinary measures for keeping the patient alive, that might be available to the patient;

(f) after being informed as referred to in paragraph (e), the patient indicates to the medical practitioner that the patient has decided to end his or her life;

(g) the medical practitioner is satisfied that the patient has considered the possible implications of the patient's decision to his or her family;

(h) the medical practitioner is satisfied, on reasonable grounds, that the patient is of sound mind and that the patient's decision to end his or her life has been made freely, voluntarily and after due consideration;

(i) the patient, or a person acting on the patient's behalf in accordance with section 9, [of the Act which provides for the need to sign a certificate of request] has, not earlier than seven days after the patient has indicated to his or her medical practitioner, signed that part of the certificate of request required to be completed by or on behalf of the patient;

(j) the medical practitioner has witnessed the patient's signature or that of the person signing on the patient's behalf, and has completed and signed the relevant declaration on the certificate;

(k) the certificate of request has been signed in the presence of the patient and the first medical practitioner by another medical practitioner, after that medical practitioner has discussed the case with the first medical practitioner and the patient and is satisfied, on reasonable grounds, that the certificate is in order, that the patient is of sound mind and the patient's decision to end his or her life has been made freely, voluntarily and after due consideration;

(l) where an interpreter is required to be present at the signing of the certificate of request, the certificate has been signed by the interpreter confirming the patient's understanding of the request for assistance;

(m) the medical practitioner has no reason to believe that he or she, the countersigning medical practitioner or a close relative or associate of either of them, will gain a financial or other advantage as a result of the death of the patient;

(n) not less than forty-eight hours has elapsed since the signing of the completed certificate of request;

(o) at no time before assisting the patient to end his or her life had the patient given to the medical practitioner an indication that it was no longer the patient's wish to end his or her life;

(p) the medical practitioner himself or herself provides the assistance and/or is and remains present while the assistance is given and until the death of the patient.

Section 5 of the Act provided, in addition, a form of conscience clause that allowed a medical practitioner to refuse to assist a patient to die. Section 8(1) of the Act provided that a medical practitioner should not assist a patient under the Act if, in his or her opinion and after considering the advice of a second medical practitioner, there were palliative care options reasonably available to the patient to alleviate the patient's pain and suffering to levels acceptable to the patient. In section 8(2) of the Act it was stated that where a patient had requested assistance under the Act and had subsequently been provided with palliative care that brought about the remission of the patient's pain or suffering, the medical practitioner should not, in pursuance of the patient's request for assistance, assist the patient under the Act. If subsequently the palliative care ceased to alleviate the patient's pain and suffering to levels acceptable to the patient, the medical practitioner could continue to assist the patient under the Act only if the patient indicated to the medical practitioner the patient's wish to proceed in pursuance of the request.

The Act made it a criminal offence for a person to give or promise any reward or advantage, or by any means to cause or threaten to cause any disadvantage, to a medical practitioner or other person for refusing to assist, or for the purpose of compelling or persuading a medical practitioner or other person to assist or refuse to assist, in the termination of a patient's life.[164] A patient could rescind a request for assistance under the Act at any time and in any manner.[165] The Act made it an offence for a person to procure the signing or witnessing of a certificate of request by deception or improper influence.[166] There were detailed provisions as to the medical records to be kept by the medical practitioner who assisted the patient. As soon as practicable after the death the medical practitioner was obliged to report the death to the coroner by sending a copy of the death certificate and so much of the medical record of the patient as related to the terminal illness and death. The coroner was obliged to advise the Attorney General of the number of patients who died under the Act and the Attorney General was to report that number to the state legislative assembly.

Action taken in accordance with the Act by a medical practitioner, or health-care provider, did not constitute an offence under that part of the criminal code including the offences of murder, manslaughter, attempted murder or aiding suicide.[167] Moreover, part IV of the Act protected medical practitioners and health-care providers acting on the instructions of the medical practitioners from the sanctions of the criminal law, from civil or criminal action or professional disciplinary action.

It was thought initially that because the Act was so heavily laden with restrictions and exceptions that in practice it would be almost impossible for a terminally ill patient to obtain assistance in dying. However, in September 1996, Bob Dent, a sixty-six-year-old Darwin resident who had suffered from prostate cancer for five years, became the first person to receive assistance in dying under the Act. However, the Rights of the Terminally Ill Act 1995 had a short and turbulent history. It was initially passed by the Northern Territory Legislative Assembly in May 1995. However, the legislation was stalled by injunctions and did not come into force until July 1996. Since then it was challenged in the Supreme Court of the Northern Territory in the case of *Wake and Gondarra v Northern Territory of Australia*[168] on the grounds that the Northern Territory's Legislative Assembly had acted beyond its powers in enacting the legislation and that the legislation had not been properly assented to. The Supreme Court of the Northern Territory did not accept this argument, finding that the power of the Northern Territory's Legislative Assembly to make laws under the Northern Territory (Self-Government) Act 1978 for the peace and good government of the Territory was broad and of the same quality as that enjoyed by the other states in Australia. The court held that it was within the power of the Northern Territory Legislative Assembly to pass legislation of this nature. The recent successful private members' bill which was debated in the Australian parliament in March 1997 terminated the Northern Territory's brief experiment in legalized euthanasia.

SLIPPERY SLOPES AND ABUSE

Opponents of active intervention to end life in the medical context have based their opposition on arguments of the slippery slope variety.[169] In the context of active euthanasia, advocates of this position hold that by allowing active euthanasia based on the patient's consent today, in the future, more invidious forms of the practice may be allowed. Thus, for example, the practice of involuntary active euthanasia may in the future gain societal acceptance as a result of the practice of active euthanasia *per se* being accepted in medical and legal codes. The following is a typical application of the slippery slope argument to the issue of active euthanasia:

> However well any legislation is hedged about with guidelines and protections against abuse, the slippery slope predicts an inevitable extension of these practices to other, more vulnerable, groups, such as those who are demented, mentally ill, chronically disabled, frail, dependent and elderly – and perhaps even simply unhappy.[170]

The classic articulation of the slippery slope argument in the context of euthanasia is to be found in the writings of the American legal academic, Professor Yale Kamisar.[171] Kamisar has argued against the introduction of laws permitting euthanasia. He raises two main objections to the introduction of legalized euthanasia. The first is based on the wedge argument. He argues that the legalization of voluntary euthanasia would lead ineluctably to the legalization of involuntary euthanasia. This is based on the premise that it is not possible to draw a rational distinction between those patients who wish to die because they are a burden to themselves and those who are euthanized because they are a burden to others.[172]

Kamisar's second objection to the legal recognition of euthanasia is the possibility of abuse or mistake. He believes that various pressures may be brought to bear on the patient by either family members or members of the medical team in whose charge the patient is, which would raise a doubt as to the validity of the patient's consent to the procedure. The interests of the patient may, as a result, be overlooked.[173]

In addition to the potential for abuse, the potential is also there for mistakes on the part of the medical practitioner. Thus, for example, a doctor may incorrectly diagnose a patient as being terminally ill. Kamisar, as a result, finds that the risk of such abuses and mistakes outweighs the competing claim of that group in society who wish to terminate their lives through euthanasia. He believes that because the class of persons who require euthanasia is so numerically insignificant, its desires should not overshadow the enormity of the potential hazards of this practice.

These arguments were countered by Glanville Williams in a 1958 article.[174] In reply to Kamisar's objection based on the wedge argument, Williams states that it would be possible for courts to establish guidelines that struck a balance between, on the one hand, the autonomy of the patient who wished to die, and, on the other, the need to prevent abuse of the kind Kamisar feared. In an earlier book, Williams outlined in detail his views on the issue of euthanasia.[175] It was this original argument which prompted Kamisar's article on euthanasia. Williams, in his book, believed that

> it is good that men should feel a horror of taking human life, but in rational judgment the quality of the life must be considered. The absolute interdiction of suicide and euthanasia involves the impossible assertion that every life, no matter what its quality or circumstances, is worth living and obligatory to be lived. This assertion of the value of mere existence, in the absence of all activities that give meaning to life, and in face of the disintegration of personality that so often follows from prolonged agony, will not stand scrutiny. On any rationally acceptable philosophy there is no ethical value in living any sort of life: the only life that is worth living is the good life.[176]

The focus is thus placed on the needs of individual patients and their circumstances rather than on the more general approach of anti-euthanasia theorists who view life *per se* as good in itself without regard to the quality of that life.

However, in the Irish context, even if it were to be accepted by the legislature or the judiciary that a right to die with assistance existed in statutory or constitutional law, would it be exercisable, given the conservative ethos of the medical profession? Even if certain hospitals allowed such procedures to take place, what of the patients who through no fault of their own find themselves in a hospital which is governed by the ethical principles of the Roman Catholic Church? Are such patients to be deprived of such a right merely through force of circumstances? That this is a sensitive issue in the Irish context is already obvious from the decision on the equally contentious issue of treatment withdrawal in *Re A Ward of Court*.[177] It is unlikely that current Irish legal thinking, while becoming increasingly liberal in the area of individual rights, will depart radically from the traditional common-law approach to active euthanasia. It is even less likely that any government will endeavour to steer through legislation on the lines of the models in either the Netherlands or the Northern Territory in Australia.

6. LEGISLATING THE RIGHT TO DIE

The development of a right-to-die jurisprudence has had a further consequence. This is the adoption by many states of living-will statutes which allow for competent persons to create a living will stating their wishes in relation to the discontinuance of life-sustaining treatment. In addition, many states have adopted durable power-of-attorney legislation which allows competent persons to appoint a particular person to make a decision on their behalf in relation to treatment withdrawal in the event of their entering a state of permanent unconsciousness.[178] Thus, in the United States, in the wake of *In Re Quinlan*[179] many states began to adopt legislative solutions to the dilemma of treatment withdrawal.

These solutions came in the form of natural-death or living-will statutes. The first state to introduce such a measure was California. The effect of the California Natural Death Act 1976[180] was to give a legal basis to the concept of an advance directive. Other states gradually followed California's lead, leading to the situation today where all fifty US states and the District of Columbia now have some form of legislation giving legal effect to the advance directive in one or other of its many forms.[181]

The generic term 'advance directive' is often used to encompass the varying forms of prospective decision-making which are of relevance to this area. As Meisel explains,

> The term 'advance directive' is used to denote several different things. First, it is sometimes used to designate the concept of anticipatory health care decision-making. At other times it is used to refer to the content of an oral or written statement made by an individual (declarant) to become effective under stated conditions. The term can also be used to refer to a vehicle for embodying such a statement, such as a living will, durable power of attorney, or other natural death act directive. (Natural death acts frequently use the terms 'directive' and 'directive to physician' as synonymous with the term 'advance directive'.)[182]

The development of the advance directive and the enduring power of attorney in the context of treatment withdrawal demonstrates an attempt on the part of policy-makers to incorporate the idea of patient autonomy into legislation. However, these forms of legal instrument by their very nature can apply only to the competent adult patient. The mentally incompetent and minors are not permitted to avail of this instrument. In addition, not all once-competent persons will have created an advance directive before entering a state of permanent unconsciousness.

Living wills are classified broadly as instruction directives. They allow the declarant (the party making the living will) to make known his or her wishes in relation to medical treatment in the event of a terminal or incurable illness. A health-care durable power of attorney falls into the category of a proxy directive. These instruments, unlike a classic living will, do not set down specific instructions in relation to medical treatment, but rather allow the principal or grantor (as the creator of the durable power of attorney is known) to appoint a proxy or proxies to make health-care decisions on his or her behalf in the event of his or her becoming incompetent.

The living will is less flexible than the health-care durable power of attorney in that at the time of framing a living will one cannot possibly contemplate all the treatment options that may be available if and when the directive becomes operative. With a durable power of attorney, the appointed surrogate will be able to judge the requirements of the particular situation contemporaneously.[183] One method of overcoming this problem is to create a combination directive which combines the advantageous aspects of both living wills and proxy directives. As Meisel has noted, 'A combination directive permits the spirit of the declarant's instructions to govern, with the interstices filled in by the proxy.'[184]

A major problem of the advance-directive legislation in the United States is its sheer diversity and lack of uniformity. This has created a situation where the rights of the terminally ill vary from one state to the next. As Roach has stated,

> Americans are now shopping for cities or states with
> more sympathetic laws on many different social and

medical issues, which creates a trend that will burden a handful of states with the most pressing and expensive problems.[185]

The case of *In Re Busalacchi*[186] illustrates the problems which beset this area. In this case the patient lay in a persistent vegetative state in a rehabilitation institution in the state of Missouri as the result of a road traffic accident. Her father sought to transfer her to Minnesota, a state which had less stringent laws in relation to treatment withdrawal. The patient had left no clear and convincing evidence of her wishes in relation to treatment withdrawal, but even if she had it is doubtful it would have proved sufficient, as she was a minor at the time of the accident and therefore lacking the competence to decide on future medical treatment. Even though her next-of-kin wished to make a treatment decision on her behalf, this was stymied by the court in its exercise of the guardianship laws. In this case it was held that the decision to move the patient was not one the parent could make without demonstrating that she was not receiving adequate care in Missouri: 'Specifically, we will not permit [a] guardian to forum shop in an effort to control whether [the patient] lives or dies.'[187]

It could be argued that this refusal might in some way interfere with the individual's right to travel. However, as Brilmayer has written,

> The home state may be able to defeat the right to travel argument by arguing that it is not preventing the woman from exercising the right to travel, but simply holding that her guardian is not entitled to make the decision for her. Here, however, we need to take a closer look at the state's guardianship law. What decisions, exactly, is the guardian ordinarily entitled to make? Assume that the state would normally allow

the guardian to move the patient from one hospital to another in order to obtain different treatment. In such circumstances the state should not be able to prohibit the guardian from moving the patient to another state on the grounds that the purpose of the move is illegal. For the purpose itself is not illegal: termination of life support would be permitted if the patient were already in that state . . .

The only argument the state can use to prevent the death would be the contention that the guardian could not decide to move the patient regardless of the illegality of the motive. One can certainly imagine states holding such a limited view of guardianship; in such states, the guardian would be prohibited from taking the patient out of the hospital for virtually any reason.[188]

However, on appeal to the Supreme Court of Missouri, it was held that the father of the patient was entitled to remove the feeding tube.[189]

Nonetheless, it is imperative that certainty should prevail in this area and various attempts have been made in the past – without particular success – to introduce a uniform approach in the law. The Uniform Rights of the Terminally Ill Act 1985[190] is a model statute drafted by the National Commissioners on Uniform State Laws. It was adopted in 1985 and forms the basis for living-will legislation in a number of states. However, it has not led to a situation of uniformity even in those states which have used it as a basis for their legislation in this area.

The Uniform Right to Refuse Treatment Act 1982 was drafted by the group Concern in Dying in 1982. This model statute provides a means by which a competent person can state how they wish to be treated in the event of their becoming incompetent and also allows them to appoint a proxy decision-maker. This Act has not been adopted by any state.[191] The Medical Treatment Decision

Act 1981 was drafted by the Society for the Right to Die in 1981. It has not been adopted by any state but has influenced certain provisions of the living-will statutes of some states.[192] These model statutes have not created a situation of greater certainty and uniformity in this area of medical treatment.

A more general difference in the approach to the question of decision-making for the incurably or terminally ill incompetent patient between the United States model and the English and Irish models is the noticeable lack of specific legislation in this field in either England or Ireland. Absent are the multifarious living-will and health-care durable power of attorney statutes which exist in the United States. Instead, it has fallen to the courts to decide in these matters.

While cases like *Airedale N.H.S. Trust v Bland*[193] and *Re A Ward of Court*[194] have given rise to a greater amount of certainty as to how to proceed in the case of the patient in a persistent or near-persistent vegetative state, these are clearly temporary measures and cannot provide the comprehensive response to the many questions which this area of medical treatment raises. Indeed, in *Re A Ward of Court* it was pointed out in the Supreme Court decision by Justice O'Flaherty that the case was not to be viewed as a general precedent:

> it is of the utmost importance to state that we are deciding this case on a specific set of facts. It must be clear that our decision should not be regarded as authority for anything wider than the case with which we are confronted.[195]

It is clear from the speeches of Lord Browne-Wilkinson and Lord Mustill in *Airedale N.H.S. Trust v Bland* that the only satisfactory solution to dilemmas of this kind is the introduction of legislation. Lord Browne-Wilkinson offered a convincing argument for a legislative solution to this dilemma:

it seems to me imperative that the moral, social and legal issues raised by this case should be considered by Parliament . . . If Parliament fails to act, then judge-made law will of necessity through a gradual and uncertain process provide a legal answer to each new question as it arises. But in my judgment that is not the best way to proceed . . .

It is for Parliament to address the wider problems which the case raises and lay down principles of law generally applicable to the withdrawal of life support systems.[196]

These concerns were echoed by Lord Mustill in his speech in *Airedale N.H.S. Trust v Bland*. He was of the opinion that

The whole matter cries out for exploration in depth by Parliament and then for the establishment by legislation not only of a new set of ethically and intellectually consistent rules, distinct from the general criminal law, but also of a sound procedural framework within which the rules can be applied to individual cases. The rapid advance of medical technology makes this an ever more urgent task, and I venture to hope that Parliament will soon take it in hand.[197]

In the wake of *Airedale N.H.S. Trust v Bland*, a number of proposals for reform have been put forward in this area of medical treatment. These shall now be examined.

THE HOUSE OF LORDS SELECT COMMITTEE MODEL FOR TREATMENT WITHDRAWAL

Following the decision in *Airedale N.H.S. Trust v Bland*, a House of Lords Select Committee was established to examine the legal and policy issues which arise in this area of medical practice. The terms of reference of the Select Committee were to examine

> the ethical, legal and clinical implications of a person's right to withhold consent to life-prolonging treatment, and the position of persons who are no longer able to give or withhold consent; and to consider whether and in what circumstances actions that have as their intention or a likely consequence the shortening of another person's life may be justified on the grounds that they accord with that person's wishes or with that person's 'best interests'; and in all the foregoing considerations to pay regard to the likely effects of changes in law or medical practice on society as a whole.[198]

The response of the House of Lords Select Committee was far from satisfactory. In its report, which was published in January 1994, the Select Committee did not recommend the introduction of specific legislation on the question of treatment withdrawal and the incompetent patient. In the place of recommending much-needed legislative guidelines in this area, the Select Committee concluded that the development of the idea that some treatments may be inappropriate and need not be given should make it unnecessary in future to consider the withdrawal of life-sustaining treatment, except where the administration of such treatment is burdensome to the patient.[199] This is unsatisfactory. Indeed, it is, in effect, a non-conclusion. As the Select Committee admitted,

> This question has caused us great difficulty, with some members of the Committee taking one view and some another, and we have not been able to reach a conclusion. But where we agreed is in judging that the question need not, indeed should not, usually be asked. In the case of Tony Bland, it might well have

been decided long before application was made to the
court that treatment with antibiotics was inappropriate,
given that recovery from the inevitable complications
of infection could add nothing to his well-being.[200]

This conclusion is of very little worth in that it presumes to
speak of a hypothetical ideal situation – what the practice ought to be
rather than what the practice is. Thus, in the wake of *Airedale N.H.S.
Trust v Bland*[201] the courts have been faced with similar applications
in relation to treatment withdrawal.[202] This call from the Select
Committee for a medical treatment idyll frankly defies explanation
and does not even attempt to resolve the problem.

The Select Committee, while welcoming the idea of the advance
directive, thought it unnecessary that legislation should be introduced on the subject.[203] This again is a flawed conclusion given the
lack of guidance which obtains at present as to the validity or
otherwise of such instruments. Instead, the Select Committee has
thrown the issue back into the hands of the courts in the great
tradition of policy hot potatoes. The justification supplied by the
Select Committee for this stance went as follows:

> We suggest that it could well be impossible to give
> advance directives in general greater legal force without
> depriving patients of the benefit of the doctor's
> professional expertise and of new treatments and
> procedures which may have become available since the
> advance directive was signed.[204]

Without appropriate statutory guidance the situation will
remain far from clear. However, it is arguable that at present an
advance directive is valid at common law. This point was made by
the Law Commission in a recent Consultation Paper when it stated
that

Following the dicta of the House of Lords in *Airedale N.H.S. Trust v Bland* it appears that it may be possible to make an advance directive which is legally binding.[205]

Thus, Lord Goff was of the view in his judgment in *Airedale N.H.S. Trust v Bland* that

> it is established that the principle of self-determination requires that respect must be given to the wishes of the patient, so that if an adult patient of sound mind refuses, however unreasonably, to consent to treatment or care by which his life would or might be prolonged, the doctors responsible for his care might give effect to his wishes, even though they do not consider it to be in his 'best interests' to do so . . . To this extent, the principle of the sanctity of human life must yield to the principle of self-determination . . . and for present purposes . . . the doctor's duty to act in the 'best interests' of his patient must likewise be qualified . . . Moreover, the same principle applies where the patient's refusal to give his consent has been expressed at an earlier date, before he became unconscious or otherwise incapable of communicating it, though in such circumstances especial care may be necessary to ensure that the prior refusal of consent is still properly to be regarded as applicable in the circumstances which have subsequently occurred.[206]

In the earlier case of *Re T (Adult: Refusal of Medical Treatment)*,[207] Lord Donaldson MR was of the view that anticipatory refusals of medical treatment will be binding provided that: (i) when the patient made such a declaration he or she was competent to consent to or to refuse treatment; (ii) that the declaration is applicable in the circumstances under review; and (iii) the declaration must not have come about as a result of undue influence.[208] The Law Commission concluded that

> In England and Wales, the dicta in *Re T (Adult: Refusal of Medical Treatment)*, together with those in *Airedale N.H.S. Trust v Bland* in both the Court of Appeal and the House of Lords indicate that an anticipatory decision which is 'clearly established' and 'applicable in the circumstances' may be as effective as the current decision of a capable adult.[209]

However, the Law Commission did not share the same faith in the existing common-law guidance as the House of Lords Select Committee, and suggested the introduction of legislation which would clarify the issues involved.[210]

The Select Committee proposed the development of a code of practice on advance directives.[211] This was also the Select Committee's response to the problems posed by the patient in a persistent vegetative state. The report stated that a definition of persistent vegetative state and a code of practice in relation to its management should be developed.[212]

This is not necessarily going to make a great impact on the immediate problem of treatment withdrawal in the case of the permanently unconscious patient. It merely leads to the setting-up of yet another committee to debate the definition of persistent vegetative state without necessarily coming to a satisfactory or indeed any solution, and seems again a means of avoiding tackling the core issues.

THE LAW COMMISSION'S MODEL FOR TREATMENT WITHDRAWAL

A more balanced and thoughtful response to the problem came in the Law Commission's Consultation Paper[213] which was published in March 1993 and in the report which followed it in March 1995.[214] The overall policy aims of the Law Commission in this area were set out in a previous Consultation Paper[215] in the following terms:

(i)   That people should be enabled and encouraged to take for themselves those decisions which they are able to take;

(ii) that where it is necessary in their own interests or for the protection of others that someone else should take decisions on their behalf, the intervention should be as limited as possible and concerned to achieve what the person himself would have wanted; and

(iii) that proper safeguards should be provided against exploitation, neglect, and physical, sexual or psychological abuse.[216]

In the report[217] the Commission modified the position in relation to point (ii), stating that

> there is no place in the scheme we recommend in this Report for the making of decisions which would protect other persons but would not be in the 'best interests' of the person without capacity.[218]

The Law Commission's proposals in relation to advance directives are straightforward. They give a statutory footing to the current common-law principles in this area as developed in the cases of *Re T (Adult: Refusal of Medical Treatment)*,[219] *Airedale N.H.S. Trust v Bland*,[220] and *In Re C (Adult: Refusal of Treatment)*.[221]

The Commission wished to codify the existing case-law and set out clearly for all concerned the law's stance on such anticipatory decisions. The Commission defined an advance refusal of treatment in the following terms for the purposes of the Draft Bill on Mental Incapacity which accompanied the report:

> an 'advance refusal of treatment' should be defined as
> a refusal made by a person aged eighteen or over with
> the necessary capacity of any medical, surgical or dental
> treatment or other procedure and intended to have
> effect at any subsequent time when he or she may be
> without capacity to give or refuse consent.[222]

The Commission did recommend, however, that an advance refusal of treatment as defined in the Draft Bill on Mental Incapacity should not preclude the provision of basic care. Basic care was defined by the Commission as 'care to maintain bodily cleanliness and to alleviate severe pain, as well as the provision of direct oral nutrition and hydration'.[223] Moreover, an advance refusal of treatment would not be applicable in the case of a pregnant woman where in such a case it endangers the life of the foetus unless the woman has previously indicated to the contrary.[224]

This sub-clause was included as a reaction to the case of *Re S (Adult: Refusal of Medical Treatment)*[225] where it was held that it was lawful for doctors to perform a Caesarean section without the consent of the woman in question. One commentator has stated that the decision in *Re S (Adult: Refusal of Medical Treatment)* seems to

> ignore what seemed to be a settled requirement for
> consent to medical treatment when the individual is
> conscious and mentally competent. Not only does the
> decision appear to ignore this, it also appears to run
> counter to the view that the foetus in English law does
> not have a legal personality until it is born alive. A belief
> in the foetus having an independent legal personality
> seems implicit in Sir Stephen Brown P.'s view that S's
> refusal of consent could be ignored; how else may an
> individual's rights be negated other than through the
> assertion, or protection, of the rights of others?[226]

The Law Commission's response, while attempting to strike a balance between the rights of the mother and those of the foetus, tends to give greater regard to those of the foetus. The Commission provided the following rationale for this position:

> We do not . . . accept that a woman's right to determine the sorts of treatment which she will tolerate somehow evaporates as soon as she becomes pregnant. There can, on the other hand, be no objection to acknowledging that many women do in fact alter their views as to the interventions they find acceptable as a direct result of the fact that they are carrying a child. By analogy with cases where life might be needlessly shortened or lost, it appears that a refusal which did not mention the possibility that the life of a foetus might be endangered would be likely to be found not to apply in circumstances where a treatment intended to save the life of the foetus was proposed. Women of child-bearing age should therefore be aware that they should address their minds to this possibility if they wish to make advance refusals of treatment.[227]

However, it could be argued that this could still lead to a situation where a woman who, for example, had neglected to state specifically her wishes in this regard, may be subjected to treatment to which she would not, if competent, consent.

Moreover, in *Re S (Adult: Refusal of Medical Treatment)*[228] the foetus in question was viable, but in the Draft Bill on Mental Incapacity the Law Commission does not specify that a woman's refusal of life-saving treatment shall be overridden only in a situation where the foetus is viable. It merely mentions the 'life of the foetus', and no more. It is to be assumed that if the foetus were not viable then efforts to save it would not be initiated. However, as Derek Morgan argues, while acknowledging that *Re S* concerned the decision of a woman with a viable foetus, no such limitation is imposed on the presumption to be introduced into the new statutory provision. Thus in line with this proposal, an unconscious pregnant woman who presents with a birth plan or advance directive which refuses active treatment in the event of, say, catastrophic brain insult, could be ventilated for the supposed benefit of an eighteen, seventeen, sixteen week or even more immature foetus.[229]

The Law Commission also recommended that medical practitioners who withhold treatment as a result of the patient's previously stated wishes shall not be held liable for the consequences. Thus, clause 9(4) of the Draft Bill on Mental Incapacity provides that

> No person shall incur any liability –
> (a) for the consequences of withholding any treatment or procedure if he has reasonable grounds for believing that an advance refusal of treatment by the person concerned applies to that treatment or procedure; or
> (b) for carrying out any treatment or procedure to which an advance refusal of treatment by the person concerned applies unless he knows, or has reasonable grounds for believing, that an advance refusal of treatment by the person concerned applies to the treatment or procedure.

The Commission also took note of those patients who may not have created an advance directive and those patients who were incapable of ever creating an advance directive due to infancy or mental incompetence. At present, the legal test applied in such cases is that stated in cases such as *Re F (Mental Patient: Sterilisation)*.[230] According to this test a doctor will not be liable when he or she treats a patient without that patient's consent where the doctor has acted in the 'best interests' of the patient and if his or her actions were in accordance with those adopted by a responsible body of medical opinion skilled in that particular field of diagnosis and treatment. The Commission favoured a more patient-centred approach. While not exactly adopting a 'substituted judgement' test in such circumstances the Commission favoured taking the patient's personality into account as far as possible. Thus, in the Consultation Paper the Commission put it in the following terms:

> a person who has never had the capacity to make decisions, or even the ability to express views, is still an individual and his unique reactions to the world may be identifiable. We consider that in determining the 'best interests' of an incapacitated adult it is appropriate to attempt to consider the consequences of a decision from the patient's point of view as far as possible.[231]

The Commission's report on mental incapacity concluded that in relation to the never-competent patient or the patient who had not created an advance directive before his incapacity, a medical practitioner should be given a statutory authority to treat provided it is reasonable in all the circumstances to safeguard the 'best interests' of an incapacitated person.[232]

In deciding whether a particular course of medical treatment is in the 'best interests' of an incapacitated patient the following criteria should be taken into account:

(1) The ascertainable past and present wishes and feelings of the person, and the factors he or she would consider,

(2) the need to permit and encourage the person to participate,

(3) the views of other appropriate people, and

(4) the availability of an effective less restrictive option.[233]

This new statutory 'best interests' test thus combines elements of both the 'best interests' and 'substituted judgement' tests as understood in United States law.

In addressing the question of the form which such advance directives should take, the Law Commission did not stipulate that they should be in writing. However, the Commission did add that there were advantages in expressing such anticipatory decisions in writing as such a step would 'be likely to furnish some definite proof that the refusal was made by the patient and intended to have effect in the future.'[234] However, the Commissioners did go on to state that

> a rebuttable presumption is the best way to balance the need for flexibility and the desirability of formal writing. It would not, of course, answer the questions the doctor must ask as to whether (1) the patient had capacity to make the refusal and whether (2) the refusal applies to the treatment now proposed and in the circumstances which now exist.[235]

In order to clarify the issue further, the Commission recommended that a code of practice in relation to advance directives be prepared. This, the Commission argued, would fill the procedural interstices which legislation could not hope to do.

While it may be considered laudable that the Commission decided to respect the spirit of the patient's wishes without constricting these wishes in evidentiary requirements, the absence of legislative guidelines on the form of an advance statement may lead to the patient's wishes not being enforced.

Indeed, it could be argued that the Commission does not succeed in striking the balance between flexibility and the need for a formal written document. While claiming that a written refusal is not required, the Commission then states that a written refusal would be likely to provide 'some definite proof'. This begs the question of what sort of proof an oral refusal would provide. Moreover, the guidelines which the Commission gives in relation to written advance statements are quite vague. The Commission states that such statements should be signed and witnessed but does not specify the number of witnesses nor does it state whether relatives of the patient should be excluded from being witnesses.

In addition to this legislative framework, the Commission has recommended a new judicial forum within which to adjudicate on such treatment decisions. The new jurisdiction would have a statutory basis. The rationale for this was stated in the following terms in the earlier Consultation Paper:

> This would overcome the limitations of the common law, by providing a range of flexible orders in addition to a jurisdiction to make declarations. We envisage that the statutory jurisdiction would have several conceptually distinct functions. First, orders might be made approving or disapproving a particular decision made on behalf of an incapacitated person, or appointing someone to make decisions on the person's behalf. Secondly, the judicial forum would exercise a declaratory jurisdiction. This would not be concerned with making decisions for the incapacitated person but with establishing and declaring the facts, for example whether a person was incapacitated, or whether an anticipatory decision was 'clearly established' and 'applicable to the circumstances'.[236]

The Law Commission also made provision for a new model of power of attorney called a 'continuing power of attorney'.[237] This model is an enhanced form of the traditional power of attorney which would allow individuals (the donors) to give legal authority to a person of their choosing (the donee) to make and implement decisions on behalf of donors when they are no longer capable through mental incapacity of making such decisions for themselves. The continuing power of attorney would apply *inter alia* to health-care decisions.[238] At present in England and Wales the power of attorney does not extend to matters other than financial affairs and property.[239]

THE BRITISH MEDICAL ASSOCIATION'S CODE OF PRACTICE ON ADVANCE STATEMENTS

The British Medical Association has recently produced a *Code of Practice* on the subject of advance statements. This initiative came about in response to the call by the House of Lords Select Committee on Medical Ethics for a code of practice in relation to advance directives for health-care professionals.

The British Medical Association, while taking a non-directive approach in relation to advance statements, nonetheless is of the view that 'carefully discussed advance statements have an important place in the development of a genuinely more balanced partnership between patients and health professionals.'[240]

The *Code of Practice* does not purport to be definitive or binding in this area of medical treatment. It is merely an example of greater 'dialogue' between parties to the therapeutic relationship. The *Code of Practice*, while welcome, also demonstrates the difficulty of allocating to professional bodies the task which should have been completed by the Law Commission, that is to say, the provision of a detailed and definitive guide to 'best practice' in this area of medical treatment. The *Code of Practice* is the result of a consultation process between the different groups and individuals with an interest in this area. It is thus, of necessity, an exercise in compromise.

Indeed, rather than fill the gaps in the Law Commission's recommendations, it seems to cause new difficulties. In relation to
the question of drafting an advance statement the *Code of Practice*
states in a similar vein to the Law Commission that

> Although oral statements are equally valid if supported
> by appropriate evidence, there are advantages to
> recording one's general views and firm decisions in
> writing. Advance statements should be understood as
> an aid to, rather than a substitute for, open dialogue
> between patients and health professionals.[241]

However, like the Law Commission, the *Code of Practice* does not
propose a sufficiently detailed scheme for the formalities to be
followed in the drawing-up of such a document. It states simply
that

> Written statements should use clear and unambiguous
> language. They should be signed by the individual and
> a witness. Model forms are available but clear statements
> in any format command respect.[242]

Thus, while being welcome in according symbolic importance to a
balanced dialogue between patient and treatment provider, and in
recognizing the concept of patient autonomy in this area, the *Code
of Practice* contains certain practical shortcomings.

THE IRISH POSITION

In Ireland, the current state of the law in the area is not
satisfactory. A logical and reasonable reaction to the decision in *Re
A Ward of Court* would be to enshrine in legislation the right of the
individual to make anticipatory decisions about treatment withdrawal. The Supreme Court, as with so many other issues of a

medico-ethical nature in Ireland, has been forced to adjudicate as a result of the failure of legislators to introduce legislation in this field, due to the fear of attracting controversy and losing votes. This failure on the part of the legislature places the judiciary in the invidious position of having to deliberate and reach solutions in highly charged moral as well as legal dilemmas. In the words of Justice McCarthy in his decision in *Attorney General v X*,[243] 'It is not for the courts to programme society; that is partly, at least, the role of the legislature. The courts are not equipped to regulate these procedures.'[244] Rather than depend on a case-by-case resolution of the dilemmas posed by treatment withdrawal, the government could decide to take some responsibility in this field and introduce a programme of legislation which would put the concept of treatment withdrawal on a statutory footing.

The first step would be to introduce legislation which would allow for the making of advance directives. This would allow those who are now competent to create a testamentary document which would set out their wishes in relation to medical treatment should they ever enter a state of incapacity.

The principal problem with this method is that those who now lack legal capacity such as the mentally incompetent and minors will be unable to avail of this instrument. Given legal conceptions of rationality and competence this problem is likely to remain.[245] On the positive side, such an initiative would at last give legal recognition to individual autonomy in this area of medical treatment, thus bringing it into line with the consent model as is understood in the case of the conscious adult and medical treatment. This, it could be argued, is merely an extension of the general right to refuse medical treatment to the area of treatment at the end of life.

The patient's wishes could still be ascertained through the medium of the advance directive. An important contribution to the debate on the introduction of legislation in this regard has been the Report of the English Law Commission[246] discussed above.

It is submitted that the Irish legislature should take a similar approach to the one outlined by the Law Commission in this area of medical practice. As our legislative canon is quite heavily influenced by English legislative conventions, this would not be a radical departure in procedural terms. The recommendations are based on a similar common-law tradition and such legislation would not prove difficult to weave into our current statutory framework. What could prove to be a difficulty would be the traditional Irish antipathy to legislation that aims to afford greater protection to individual autonomy.

A complementary form of legislation which could also be introduced is the idea of a health-care enduring power of attorney. In Ireland the law in relation to powers of attorney is contained in the Powers of Attorney Act 1996. This Act provides, *inter alia*, for the creation of an enduring power of attorney. This form of power of attorney allows the power to endure after the donor of the power has become mentally incapacitated. However, the enduring power of attorney extends only to property, business or financial affairs and personal-care decisions. Section 4 of the Act defines personal-care decisions as follows:

   (a) where the donor should live,

   (b) with whom the donor should live,

   (c) whom the donor should see and not see,

   (d) what training or rehabilitation the donor should get,

   (e) the donor's diet and dress,

   (f) inspection of the donor's personal papers,

   (g) housing, social welfare and other benefits for the donor.

Decisions in relation to health care or medical treatment are not included within the ambit of the enduring power of attorney as currently understood.

The principal obstacle to the legal recognition of a health-care power of attorney in the case of a patient who, for example, enters a permanent state of unconsciousness or the introduction of living-will legislation would appear to be government reluctance to recognize that a detailed statutory framework is required to deal with the complex issues of fact and law that may arise in this area of medical treatment.

7. CONCLUSION

There is a choice to be made as to the model which will form the basis for legal intervention in the area of death and dying in Ireland. On the one hand, one can choose the model of the natural death. This model is rooted in deontological ideas about the intrinsic value of life as an abstract ideal. The natural death model is the offspring of the sanctity of life model and is thus absolutist and impersonal. The sanctity of life model has been the dominant model in Irish legal discourse on the topic of the right to life to date. This model, rather than being a flexible one, adapting to the needs of an evolving societal framework, is absolutist. In other words, it fits into Ronald Dworkin's model of the 'constitution of detail'.[247] This model is hardly the model which would fit very easily into the medical law context. Medical law is concerned with often quite complex fact situations involving, *inter alia*, important questions of personal autonomy. As a result, the wishes and desires of the individual patient must be taken into account, not in a perfunctory manner, but in a manner which best serves the autonomy of the patient, while not forgetting the interests of the health-care provider. Applying a deontological model to this scenario may serve the purpose of upholding the ideal of the sanctity of life, but it does not uphold the equally important ideal of patient autonomy.

That this model poorly serves individual autonomy can be seen in the manner in which both the courts and the legislature have dealt with issues in the sphere of medical practice. Thus, the issue of abortion demonstrated clearly the important practical ramifications of applying a deontological model to a question of individual autonomy. The patient and doctor, the central participants in this therapeutic relationship, have within this model been relegated to the status of mere bit-players, performing roles which are neither respectful of individual autonomy nor dignity of the person.

In recent years, this deontological model has been subject to challenge from another model which appears to offer more in terms of respecting individual autonomy. Thus, having witnessed the case of *Attorney General v X and Others*[248] and that of *Re A Ward of Court*,[249] one could argue that Irish law in the zone of individual rights may be commencing to question the previous paradigm of the sanctity of life in more vehement terms than heretofore.

It could be argued that, like Irish society, Irish law in this zone is undergoing a difficult metamorphosis from the paradigm of the natural to that of the post-natural. What the post-natural phase of Irish individual rights jurisprudence holds will be dependent on individuals rather than on the moral collectivity. It is to be hoped that the transition will lead to a new autonomy, this time personal rather than political.

This alternative model has much in common with the rights model as defined by Dworkin[250] and interpreted by Brock[251] in the medical context. In constitutional terms this model would fit into Dworkin's model of the 'constitution of principle'.[252] This model, it is submitted, leads in practical terms to a more equitable resolution of the dilemmas which arise in the area of death and dying.

That it is important to identify a model which will underpin any future Irish jurisprudence on death is clear. The phenomenon of the legal appropriation of death is a societal reality from which Ireland is not immune. In the face of the very real policy and personal ramifications of the issues that arise from this phenomenon, how have legal and policy actors in Ireland reacted? It has to be said not very well. The country has, in effect, no policy framework within which to resolve the complex dilemmas in this area of medical practice.

The Supreme Court's decision in *Re A Ward of Court* has accelerated the need for a legislative response to the question of treatment withdrawal, by putting in place legislation in the area of advance directives which would give legal reality to the ideal of individual autonomy at life's end. Detailed legislative guidance on the issue is crucial, both for the patient and for the health-care professional who is faced with such dilemmas daily.

The issue of active intervention to end life seems for many to be beyond the pale of acceptable medical practice. The sanctity of life model would not allow of such a development. However, the Netherlands and, briefly, the Northern Territory in Australia have accepted as part of medical practice active euthanasia and physician-assisted suicide. This is reflective of an alternative conception of the sanctity of life which accepts that a time will come in the lives of many when the greatest respect which can be accorded them is to respect their wish to die, or as Garcia Marquez has put it, 'to help them die without fear of pain'.[253]

Irish medical jurisprudence is currently in a developmental phase. The way in which those who shape policy confront this topic will affect all parties to the therapeutic relationship. If we choose to do nothing, and wait until the dilemmas present themselves before the courts, then the result is uncertainty, both for patients who are unaware of their rights in the therapeutic relationship and for doctors who are unsure of the limits of their duties. The most logical and, indeed, equitable solution to this problem is to provide a legislative solution. This would clearly delineate the rights and responsibilities of all parties to the relationship.

How is such legislation to be informed? Is it to be informed by a deontological model which would hardly accommodate patient or professional autonomy, or is it to be informed by a model based on individual rights? The most equitable basis for such legislation is a rights model. This model would respect the autonomy of both doctor and patient. Moreover, unlike the deontological model, it is unhindered by the difficulty of imposing absolutist models on rapidly advancing and complex fact situations.

The alternative model would facilitate a shift from a societal paradigm, where, as Outram has explained,

> the body appears . . . as a place where the ability to control is overwhelmingly made manifest. Such a control – until very recently – has made attitudes to the body a touchstone of social conformity[254]

to a paradigm where policy would uphold

> the dignity and identity of all human beings and guarantee everyone, without discrimination, respect for their integrity and other rights and fundamental freedoms with regard to the application of biology and medicine.[255]

Notes and References

1. Aries, P., *The Hour of Our Death* (New York: Alfred A. Knopf, 1981), pp. 5–20.
2. Ibid.
3. Ibid., p. 19.
4. Ibid., p. 559.
5. See further Sheehy, N., '"Talk about being Irish": Death ritual as a cultural forum' (1994), 15, *Irish Journal of Psychology*, pp. 494–503.
6. See generally O'Suilleabhain, S., *Irish Wake Amusements* (Cork: The Mercier Press, 1967).
7. Sheehy, N., op. cit., p. 500.
8. Ibid., p. 503.
9. Ibid., p. 502.
10. Ibid., pp. 505–6.
11. Aries, P., op. cit., pp. 584–5.
12. Ibid., p. 588.
13. Callahan, D., *The Troubled Dream of Life: Living with Mortality* (New York: Simon and Schuster, 1993), pp. 11–22.
14. Ibid., p. 35.
15. Ibid., p. 36.
16. Ibid.
17. Ibid., p. 225.
18. Ibid., p. 67.
19. Ibid.
20. Dworkin, R., *Taking Rights Seriously* (London: Duckworth, 1984), p. 171.
21. See Aquinas, T., *Summa Theologiae*, vol. 38 (London: Blackfriars/ Eyre and Spottiswoode, 1975), p. 43.
22. See further Beauchamp, T., and Childress, J., *Principles of Biomedical Ethics*, 3rd edn. (New York: Oxford University Press, 1989), pp. 127–34.
23. See generally Glover, J., *Causing Death and Saving Lives* (Harmondsworth: Penguin, 1990), p. 87; Tomkin, D., and Hanafin, P., *Irish Medical Law* (Dublin: Round Hall Press, 1995), pp. 149–54.
24. Aquinas, T., op. cit., p. 23.
25. Aquinas, T., *Summa Theologiae*, vol. 35 (London: Blackfriars/Eyre and Spottiswoode, 1972), pp. 81–5.

26. Dworkin, R., op. cit., p. 174.

27. For further analysis see Clarke, D.M., 'The Constitution and the natural law: A reply to Mr Justice O'Hanlon' (1993), 11, *Irish Law Times*, pp. 177–8; Costello, D., 'The natural law and the Irish Constitution' (1956), 45, *Studies*, pp. 403–7; Murphy, T. 'Democracy, natural law and the Irish Constitution' (1993), 11, *Irish Law Times*, pp. 81–3.

28. Henchy, S., 'Precedent in the Irish Supreme Court' (1962), 25, *Modern Law Review*, p. 557.

29. See Costello, D., op. cit., pp. 403–5; Henchy, S., op. cit., p. 557; O'Hanlon, R.J., 'Natural rights and the Irish Constitution' (1993), 11, *Irish Law Times*, pp. 8–10.

30. O'Hanlon, R.J., op. cit., p. 10.

31. Cited by Sheehy, G., 'The right to marry in the Irish tradition of the common law', in O'Reilly, J. (ed.), *Human Rights and Constitutional Law: Essays in Honour of Brian Walsh* (Dublin: Round Hall Press, 1992), p. 22.

32. See O'Hanlon, R.J., op. cit., pp. 8–10.

33. [1992] 1 I.R. 1.

34. O'Hanlon, R.J., op. cit., p. 8.

35. Ibid.

36. Ibid., p. 10.

37. [1992] 1 I.R. 1.

38. See further Corwin, E., 'The "Higher Law" background of American constitutional law' (1928–29), 42, *Harvard Law Review*, p. 149 and p. 365 (in two parts).

39. See Dworkin, R., *Freedom's Law: The Moral Reading of the American Constitution* (Oxford: Oxford University Press, 1996).

40. Feldman, D., *Civil Liberties and Human Rights in England and Wales* (Oxford: Clarendon Press, 1993), p. 364.

41. Dworkin, R., *Life's Dominion: An Argument about Abortion and Euthanasia* (London: HarperCollins, 1993), p. 119.

42. Dworkin, R., op. cit at n.1 *supra*, p. 171.

43. Ibid., p. 172.

44. Brock, D., *Life and Death: Philosophical Essays in Biomedical Ethics* (Cambridge: Cambridge University Press, 1993), p. 97.

45. Ibid.

46. Ibid., pp. 99–100.

47. Ibid., p. 99.

48. Ibid., p. 100.

49. Ibid., p. 99.

50. Admiraal, P., 'Voluntary euthanasia: The Dutch way', in McLean, S.A.M. (ed.), *Death, Dying and the Law* (Aldershot: Dartmouth, 1996), p. 123.

51. Mason, J.K., 'Death and dying: One step at a time?', in McLean, S.A.M., op. cit., p. 162.

52. [1993] 2 W.L.R. 316.

53. Ibid., p. 387.

54. Note, 'Physician-assisted suicide and the right to die with assistance' (1992), 105, *Harvard Law Review*, pp. 2021–40.

55. Ibid., pp. 2029–31.

56. See Meisel, A., *The Right to Die* (New York: John Wiley and Sons, 1989), p. 78.

57. Costello, D., 'The terminally ill – The law's concerns' (1986), 21, *Irish Jurist*, pp. 35–46.

58. Ibid., p. 42.

59. Ibid.

60. Ibid., p. 44.

61. Rachels, J., 'Active and passive euthanasia' (1975), 292, *New England Journal of Medicine*, pp. 78–80.

62. Ibid., p. 79.

63. Ibid., p. 80.

64. Ibid.

65. Feinberg, J., *The Moral Limits of the Criminal Law: Harm to Others* vol.1 (New York: Oxford University Press, 1984), pp. 165–85.

66. Ibid., p. 166.

67. [1995] 2 I.L.R.M. 401.

68. Ibid., p. 419.

69. Ibid., pp. 418–19.

70. President's Commission for the Study of Ethical Problems in Medicine and Biomedical and Behavioral Research, *Deciding to Forego Life-Sustaining Treatment: A Report on the Ethical, Medical, and Legal Issues in Treatment Decisions* (Washington: Government Printing Office, 1983), p. 135.

71. See Meisel, A., op. cit., p. 264.

72. See Gaylin, W., and Macklin, R., *Who Speaks for the Child?* (New York: Plenum Press, 1982).

73. See for example *Re F (Mental Patient: Sterilisation)* [1989] 2 All E.R. 545.
74. Meisel, A., op. cit., p. 266.
75. *In Re Conservatorship of Orabnick* 109 S.Ct. 399 (1988).
76. 357 N.W. 2d 332 (Minn. 1984).
77. Note, op. cit., at n.54 *supra*, p. 1653.
78. [1993] 2 W.L.R. 316.
79. Ibid., p. 333.
80. Ibid., p. 396.
81. [1989] 2 All E.R. 545.
82. *Airedale N.H.S. Trust v Bland* [1993] 2 W.L.R. 316, p. 371.
83. Ibid., pp. 385–6.
84. Ibid., p. 398.
85. Ibid.
86. Kennedy, I., and Grubb, A., 'Withdrawal of artificial hydration and nutrition: Incompetent adult' (1993), 1, *Medical Law Review*, pp. 359–70.
87. Ibid., pp. 362–3.
88. The origins of the doctrine of 'substituted judgement' lie in the decision of Lord Eldon in *Ex Parte Whitbread* (1816) 2 Meriv. 99, 35 Eng. Rep. 878 Ch.
89. *In Re Eichner* 426 N.Y.S. 2d 517 (1980), p. 548. For a detailed critique of the doctrine see Buchanan, A., and Brock, D., *Deciding for Others: The Ethics of Surrogate Decison-making* (Cambridge: Cambridge University Press, 1989), pp. 112–22.
90. 355 A.2d 647 (N.J.) (1976).
91. Harmon, L., 'Falling off the vine: Legal fictions and the doctrine of substituted judgement' (1990), 100, *Yale Law Journal*, pp. 37–8.
92. See for example *Brophy v New England Sinai Hospital, Inc.* 497 N.E. 2d 626; *In Re Spring* 405 N.E. 2d 115 (1980); *Superintendent of Belchertown State School v Saikewicz* 370 N.E. 2d 417 (1977).
93. See Meisel, A., op. cit., pp. 275–7.
94. See further note, op. cit., at n.54 *supra*, pp. 1649–51.
95. See further Teff, H., *Reasonable Care: Legal Perspectives on the Doctor–Patient Relationship* (Oxford: Clarendon Press, 1994), pp. 41.
96. Costello, R., 'Supreme Court decision "a clear case of euthanasia"', *Cork Examiner*, 28 July 1995, p. 4.
97. See Irish Medical Council, 'Statement of the Council after their statutory meeting on 4th August, 1995' (Dublin: The Medical Council,

1995); Irish Nursing Board, 'Guidance of the Irish Nursing Board of 18th August, 1995' (Dublin: The Nursing Board, 1995).

98. Irish Medical Council, op. cit.

99. Irish Medical Council, *A Guide to Ethical Conduct and to Fitness to Practise* (Dublin: The Medical Council, 1994), para. 12.05.

100. [1992] 1 I.R. 1.

101. Irish Medical Council, op. cit., at n.101 *supra*, p. 36.

102. See Tomkin, D,, and Hanafin, P., *Irish Medical Law* (Dublin: Round Hall Press, 1995), pp. 185–6; Whitty, N., 'Law and the regulation of reproduction in Ireland, 1922–1992' (1993), 43, *University of Toronto Law Journal*, p. 887.

103. See further Girvin, B., 'Social change and political culture in the Republic of Ireland' (1993), 46, *Parliamentary Affairs*, pp. 380–98.

104. See for example *McGee v Attorney General* [1974] I.R. 284; *Attorney General v X* [1992] 1 I.R. 1.

105. Girvin, B., op. cit., p. 389.

106. O'Leary, C., and Hesketh, T., 'The Irish abortion and divorce referendum campaigns' (1988), 3, *Irish Political Studies*, p. 59.

107. [1995] 2 I.L.R.M. 401, pp. 453–4.

108. See further Pearce, R. 'Abortion and the right to life under the Irish Constitution' (1993), 15, *Journal of Social Welfare and Family Law*, p. 400.

109. See Mason, J.K., and McCall-Smith, R.A., *Law and Medical Ethics*, 4th edn. (London: Butterworths, 1994), p. 429.

110. However, some commentators insist that there is essentially no difference between the two concepts. See further Fletcher, J., *Morals and Medicine* (Boston: Beacon Press, 1954), p. 176; Barrington, M. 'Apologia for suicide', in Downing, A.B. (ed.), *Euthanasia and the Right to Death: The Case for Voluntary Euthanasia* (Atlantic Highlands, New Jersey: Humanities Press, 1969), p. 162; Gillon, R., 'Suicide and voluntary euthanasia: Historical perspectives', in Downing, A.B., op. cit., pp. 173–4.

111. Quill, T.E., Cassel, C.K., and Meier, D.E., 'Proposed clinical criteria for physician-assisted suicide', in Blank, R.H., and Bonnicksen, A.L. (eds), *Medicine Unbound: The Human Body and the Limits of Medical Intervention* (New York: Columbia University Press, 1994), pp. 190–1.

112. [1995] 2 I.L.R.M. 401.

113. Ibid., p. 423.

114. Costello, D., op. cit., p. 42.

115. Ibid., p. 42.

116. Revised Code of Washington Annotated, sections 70.122.100– .905 (1992).

117. Cited by Annas, G., 'Death by prescription: The Oregon initiative' (1994), 331, *New England Journal of Medicine*, p. 1240.

118. *Compassion in Dying v Washington* 850 F. Supp. 1454 (D.C. Wash.) (1994).

119. 112 S.Ct 2791 (1992).

120. *Compassion in Dying v Washington* 850 F.Supp. 1454 (D.C. Wash.) (1994), pp. 1459–60.

121. *Planned Parenthood v Casey* 112 S.Ct. 2791 (1992), p. 2806.

122. 850 F.Supp. 1454 (D.C Wash.) (1994), p. 1460.

123. 110 S.Ct. 2841 (1990).

124. 850 F.Supp. 1454 (D.C. Wash.) (1994), p. 1461.

125. Ibid.

126. The Fourteenth Amendment to the Constitution was ratified in 1868. The Equal Protection Clause is to be found in Section 1 of the Fourteenth Amendment. It provides that no state shall 'deny to any person within its jurisdiction the equal protection of the laws'.

127. See for example *In Re Guardianship of Bowman* 617 P.2d 731 (1980).

128. 850 F.Supp. 1454 (D.C. Wash.) (1994), pp. 1466–7.

129. 112 S.Ct. 2791 (1992), p. 2830.

130. 850 F.Supp. 1454 (D.C. Wash.) (1994), p. 1465.

131. Ibid.

132. Ibid., p. 1466.

133. *Compassion in Dying v Washington* 49 F.3d 586 (9th Cir.) (1995).

134. Quill, T.E., 'Death and dignity – a case of individualized decision-making' (1991), 324, *New England Journal of Medicine*, pp. 691–4.

135. *Quill v Koppel* 870 F.Supp. 78 (1994).

136. *Quill v Vacco* No. 95–7028 (United States Court of Appeal for the Second Circuit) (1996).

137. Ibid., p. 13.

138. The Law Reform Commission of Canada, *Euthanasia, Aiding Suicide and Cessation of Treatment* (Ottawa: Minister of Supply and Services Canada, 1982), p. 53.

139. Ibid., p. 54.

140. The Law Reform Commission of Canada, *Report on Euthanasia, Aiding Suicide and Cessation of Treatment* (Ottawa: Minister of Supply and Services Canada, 1983), pp. 29–35.

141. (1994) 107 D.L.R. (4th) 342.

142. A condition also known as amyotrophic lateral sclerosis, which leaves the sufferer unable to speak, swallow, walk or move her body without assistance. In the later stages of the disease, the sufferer loses the ability to breathe without the aid of a respirator or to eat without the aid of a gastronomy tube.

143. Section 7 provides:
Everyone has the right to life, liberty and security of the person and the right not to be deprived thereof except in accordance with the principles of fundamental justice.
Section 12 provides:
Everyone has the right not to be subjected to any cruel and unusual treatment or punishment.
Section 15(1) provides:
Every individual is equal before and under the law and has the right to the equal protection and equal benefit of the law without discrimination and, in particular, without discrimination, based on race, national or ethnic origin, colour, religion, sex, age or mental or physical disability.

144. (1994) 107 D.L.R. (4th) 342, p. 356.

145. Ibid., p. 406.

146. See *Ciarlariello v Schacter* (1993) 100 D.L.R. (4th) 609; *Nancy B v Hotel-Dieu de Quebec* (1992) 86 D.L.R. (4th) 285.

147. (1994) 107 D.L.R. (4th) 342, p. 405.

148. Silving, H., 'Euthanasia: A study in comparative criminal law' (1954), 103, *University of Pennsylvania Law Review*, p. 354.

149. Wolhandler, S., 'Voluntary active euthanasia for the terminally ill and the constitutional right to privacy' (1984), 69, *Cornell Law Review*, p. 369.

150. See Fenigsen, R., 'The Netherlands: New regulations concerning euthanasia' (1993), 9, *Issues in Law and Medicine*, pp. 167–73.

151. *Rules concerning assistance rendered by a physician who pleads higher necessity when terminating life of a patient upon his explicit and serious request*, Tweede Kamer der Staten-Generaal, Vergaderjaar 1987– 1988, nos. 1–2, 20 383, pp. 1–3.

152. See van der Maas, P., van Delden, J., and Pijnenborg, L., *Euthanasia and other Medical Decisions concerning the End of Life: An Investigation performed upon request of the Commission of Enquiry into the medical practice concerning euthanasia* (The Hague: Central Bureau of Statistics, 1991).

153. Nederlandse Jurisprudentie (1985) no. 106, 451.

154. The defence of necessity in Dutch law is to be found in Article 40 of the Penal Code 1891. This provides that a person who has committed an offence due to either necessity or irresistible compulsion shall not be liable for that offence. The defence takes either of two forms. The act may have been committed as a result of psychological compulsion or it may have been perpetrated as the result of an emergency where the accused breaks the law in the interests of what he considers to be a greater or higher good. In the case of *Office of Public Prosecutions v Leendert*, the latter form of the defence was accepted by the Supreme Court. In that case the doctor concerned was of the opinion that a greater good would be served by terminating the patient's life, that is to say, ending her pain and suffering.

155. Nederlandse Jurisprudentie (1985) no.106, 451, p. 453.

156. Ibid.

157. Keown, J., 'The law and practice of euthanasia in The Netherlands' (1992), 108, *Law Quarterly Review*, p. 55.

158. See further Leenen, H.J.J., 'Dying with dignity: Developments in the field of euthanasia in the Netherlands' (1989), 8, *Medical Law*, pp. 517–26.

159. Nederlandse Jurisprudentie (1994) no. 656, 3142.

160. See Keown, op. cit., pp. 57–61.

161. The Royal Dutch Medical Association, 'Guidelines for euthanasia' (1988), 3, *Issues in Law and Medicine*, pp. 429–31.

162. *Rules concerning assistance rendered by a physician who pleads higher necessity when terminating life of a patient upon his explicit and serious request*, Tweede Kamer der Staten-Generaal, Vergaderjaar 1987–1988, nos. 1–2, 20 383, pp. 1–3.

163. Section 3.

164. Section 6(1).

165. Section 10(1).

166. Section 11(1).

167. Section 16.

168. No. 112 (Supreme Court of the Northern Territory) (1996).

169. See Ogilvie, A.D., and Potts, S.G., 'Assisted suicide for depression: The slippery slope in action?' (1994), 309, *British Medical Journal*, pp. 492–3.

170. Ibid., p. 493.

171. See Kamisar, Y., 'Some non-religious views against proposed "mercy-killing" legislation' (1958), 42, *Minnesota Law Review*, pp. 969–98; Kamisar, Y., 'When is there a constitutional "right to die"? When is there no constitutional "right to live"? (1991), 25, *Georgia Law Review*, pp. 1203–42.

172. Kamisar, Y., op. cit. 2 (1958), p. 987.

173. Ibid., p. 997.

174. Williams, G., '"Mercy-killing" legislation – a rejoinder' (1958), 43, *Minnesota Law Review*, p. 1.

175. Williams, G., *The Sanctity of Life and the Criminal Law* (London: Faber and Faber), pp. 277–312.

176. Ibid., pp. 281–2.

177. [1995] 2 I.L.R.M. 401.

178. See further Roach, C.A., 'Paradox and Pandora's Box: The tragedy of current right to die jurisprudence' (1991), 25, *University of Michigan Journal of Law Reform*, pp. 161–8.

179. 355 A.2d 647 (N.J.) (1976).

180. California Health and Safety Code sections 7185–7195 (1976).

181. See further King, N.P.M., *Making Sense of Advance Directives* (Dordrecht: Kluwer Academic Publishers, 1992).

182. Meisel,A., op. cit., p. 318.

183. See Meisel, A., op. cit., pp. 318–35.

184. Ibid., p. 322.

185. Roach, C.A., op. cit., p. 166.

186. 5 March 1991, no. 59582, 1991 Mo. App. LEXIS 315.

187. Ibid., p. 17.

188. Brilmayer, L., 'Interstate pre-emption: The right to travel, the right to life, and the right to die' (1993), 91, *Michigan Law Review*, p. 905.

189. Ibid., p. 874.

190. 9B Uniform Laws Annotated 609 (1987).

191. Meisel, A., op. cit., p. 336.

192. Ibid.

193. [1993] 2 W.L.R. 316.

194. [1995] 2 I.L.R.M. 401.

195. [1995] 2 I.L.R.M. 401, p. 431. See also the judgments of Chief Justice Hamilton at p. 423 and Justice Blayney at p. 444.

196. [1993] 2 W.L.R. 316, p. 382.

197. Ibid., p. 392.

198. House of Lords Select Committee on Medical Ethics, *Report of the Select Committee on Medical Ethics* (London: HMSO, 1994), p. 7.

199. Ibid., para. 257.

200. Ibid.

201. [1993] 2 W.L.R. 316.

202. See for example *Re G* (1995) *Med.L.Rev.* 80.

203. House of Lords Select Committee on Medical Ethics, op. cit., paras. 263–4.

204. Ibid., para. 264.

205. The Law Commission, *Consultation Paper on Mentally Incapacitated Adults and Decision-Making: Medical Treatment and Research* (London: HMSO, 1993), para. 264.

206. [1993] 2 W.L.R. 316, p. 367.

207. [1992] 3 W.L.R. 782.

208. Ibid., p. 798.

209. The Law Commission, op. cit. (1993), para. 3.7.

210. Ibid., paras. 3.11–3.20.

211. House of Lords Select Committee on Medical Ethics, op. cit., paras. 265–7.

212. Ibid., para. 258.

213. The Law Commission, op. cit. (1993), para. 3.11.

214. The Law Commission, *Report on Mental Incapacity* (London: HMSO, 1995), paras. 5.1–5.39.

215. The Law Commission, *Mentally Incapacitated Adults and Decision-Making: An Overview* (London: HMSO, 1991), para. 4.27.

216. Ibid.

217. The Law Commission, op. cit. (1995), para. 2.46.

218. Ibid.

219. [1992] 3 W.L.R. 782.

220. [1993] 2 W.L.R. 316.

221. [1994] 1 W.L.R. 290.

222. The Law Commission, op. cit. (1995), para. 516.

223. Ibid., para. 5.36.

224. Ibid., para 5.26.
225. [1992] 4 All E.R. 671.
226. Thomson, M., 'After *Re S*' (1994), 2, *Medical Law Review*, p. 130.
227. The Law Commission, op. cit. (1995), para. 5.25.
228. [1992] 4 All E.R. 671.
229. Morgan, D. 'On mental incapacity' (1995), 145, *New Law Journal*, p. 352.
230. [1989] 2 All E.R. 545.
231. The Law Commission, op. cit. (1993), para. 3.50.
232. Draft Bill on Mental Incapacity, clauses 4(1) and 3(1).
233. The Law Commission, op. cit. (1995), para. 5.7.
234. Ibid., para. 5.29.
235. Ibid., para. 5.30.
236. The Law Commission, op. cit. (1993), para. 4.4.
237. The Law Commission, op. cit., (1995).
238. Draft Bill on Mental Incapacity, clause 16(1).
239. See section 3(1) of the *Enduring Powers of Attorney Act* 1985.
240. British Medical Association, *Advance Statements about Medical Treatment: Code of Practice* (London: British Medical Association, 1995), p. 1.
241. Ibid., para. 6.1.
242. Ibid., para. 6.2.
243. [1992] 1 I.R. 1.
244. Ibid., p. 83.
245. See The Law Commission, op. cit. (1995), para. 5.18.
246. Ibid., paras. 5.1–5.39.
247. Dworkin, R., op. cit. (1993), p. 119.
248. [1992] 1 I.R. 1.
249. [1995] 2 I.L.R.M. 401.
250. Dworkin, R., op. cit. (1984), p. 171.
251. Brock, D., op. cit., pp. 95–122.
252. Dworkin, R. op. cit. (1993), p. 119.
253. Garcia Marquez, G., *Love in the Time of Cholera*, trans. Grossman, E. (London: Jonathan Cape, 1988), p. 14.
254. Outram, D., 'Negating the natural: Or why Irish historians deny science' (1986), 1, *Irish Review*, p. 47.
255. Council of Europe, *Draft Convention for the Protection of Human Rights and Dignity of the Human Being with regard to the Application of Biology and Medicine: Bioethics Convention* (Strasbourg: Council of Europe Directorate of Legal Affairs, 1994), Article 1.